LOST AMERICAN PROJECTS
A SPACECRAFT MODELLER'S GUIDE

LOST AMERICAN PROJECTS

A SPACECRAFT MODELLER'S GUIDE

Mat Irvine

With Historical Context by David Baker

⁙ THE CROWOOD PRESS

CONTENTS

INTRODUCTION

This book is intended to be a follow-on to my original book published by The Crowood Press Ltd, *Scale Spacecraft Modelling*, but this time there are detailed descriptions of what could have been built, from my colleague David Baker. It is intended for modellers who have at least a passing knowledge of model building. *Scale Spacecraft Modelling* featured in detail many aspects of building models of spacecraft and rockets, including information on the types of tools and paint required, working environments and other aspects such as spray painting, applying decals and scratch-building additional parts. Consequently these minutiae are not repeated here – the recommendation, somewhat obviously, is to please read the earlier book!

However, there are some aspects that come up fairly frequently in this book, that perhaps do need a little further explanation.

As this book features spacecraft that were planned, but not built, there are no commercial model kits of them. But all were based around craft that had been designed, built and launched, and for which commercial model kits have been made. So the starting point for many of the builds included here can start with an existing kit.

Because of the subject matter, the numbers of the kits used here do get repeated, but most should be reasonably easily to obtain, if not from one manufacturer, then maybe from another. Plus many modellers still have stashes of unbuilt kits tucked away (invariably referred to as 'loft insulation'), so these can finally have a use! It could also be a time to dig out old, already built kits that maybe have seen better days and perhaps should have been consigned to the dustbin or garbage can. But recycling is all the rage, and anyway most modellers are extremely reluctant to throw anything away – 'You never know, it might come in useful...' – and these conversions may indeed be the chance to prove that point.

Of course the model kit industry does not stand still, and although all the model kits in these conversions have been available at some time or another, and may even still be widely available when this book is published, it does not mean that they will be forever. But new kits of the same subject get issued, and old kits frequently get reissued. And local model clubs still run shows and swap-meets, where modellers have tables full of their old stock of kits that they will 'never get round to building', so sell them off (then invariably spend the cash on buying yet more kits from fellow modellers on other stands, so the stock never really diminishes...). In addition there is the joy (or otherwise) of those on-line auction sites where obsolete kits can be obtained, some still at amazingly reasonable prices.

Here is a short list of the main kits used in these conversions, and where there are alternatives.

MODEL KIT CONVERSIONS

Saturn V

In the 1:144 scale used here for the conversions, the two mainly available kits of the Apollo Saturn V are from Airfix and Monogram. (The latter is now under the Revell name, but it is the same kit.) In more

Revell 1:144-scale Apollo Saturn V. This is the reboxing of the Monogram kit.

Airfix 1:144-scale Apollo Saturn V – early box.

Airfix 1:144-scale Skylab Saturn V.

Monogram 1:144 Apollo Saturn V – first box.

recent years 4D issued a 'visible' 1:144-scale Saturn V, though the Airfix and Monogram/Revell are going to be easier to find and cheaper, even at today's prices.

But if you wish to adapt the scales of the builds using the Saturn V, there is one from AMT that is down in scale to 1:200, and up in scale there is the 1:96 example from Revell. Even larger is the newest kit from Dragon, in 1:72 scale. Airfix also makes the Skylab Saturn V in 1:144, and Dragon makes it in 1:72, where most of the parts are the same as the Apollo version.

Saturn IB

The main kit here is the Airfix one in 1:144 scale, but AMT makes one in 1:200 scale in its 'Man in Space' five-rocket set, and Dragon makes one in 1:72. There are also resin versions in 1:144, from RealSpace Models and New Ware.

Space Shuttle

The conversions here use 1:144 scale, and most use the Airfix kit. However, Revell also makes a similar 1:144 kit. Both companies make this as the Full Stack set-up, so with Solid Rocket Boosters (SRBs), External Tank (ET) and the Orbiter itself. In fact Airfix only makes this set-up, while Revell makes separate Orbiter and full stack kits. A full stack kit is also made by Minicraft. (This started life as a G-Mark kit, then Entex, now Minicraft, but the kits are

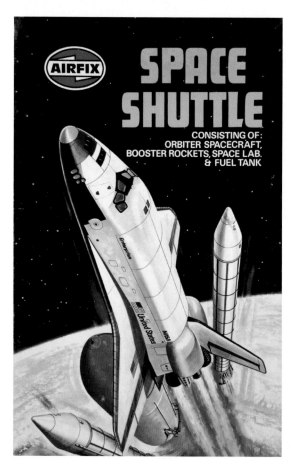

Airfix 1:144-scale Saturn IB – box for the third issue.

Airfix 1:144-scale Full Stack Space Shuttle – first box (with some technical issues – these are corrected in later box-art).

Revell 1:144-scale Full Stack Space Shuttle – one of a number of issues.

Revell 1:144-scale Space Shuttle Orbiter – one of a number of issues.

Hasegawa and Lindberg make full stack Shuttles in 1:200 scale; the latter was also available under the AMT name. (As AMT also makes the 1:200 'Man in Space' set, it makes this transfer of name somewhat logical.) Then there are even smaller-scale Shuttle full stack kits in 1:288 scale, originating from Union and Academy. The Union kits have also been issued under other names, such as Revell and Doyusha. These have been available as full stack, Orbiter only, and with a 747 as the SCA. (If you are wondering as to the 'oddness' of this scale, it came about as it is half of 1:144, itself half of the traditional aircraft scale of 1:72.)

Apollo

Revell has made the most of Apollo over the years, with kits in 1:96 and 1:48 scales. The 1:48 especially is used a great deal in these conversions, as although from very early years, and based on 'boiler-plate' mock-ups, it does still look the part, and has many useful parts for these conversions. Monogram and Dragon have also made good use of Apollo, and the Monogram 1:48-scale Lunar Module and the 1:32 Command Service Module (CSM) find their way into these pages. The 1:72-scale Airfix Apollo Lunar Module is also a source of parts.

identical, though the moulding colours can vary.) A 1:144-scale Shuttle Orbiter has been made by Bandai (now a rare kit), and Dragon makes an Orbiter by itself, and also with the Boeing 747 SCA (Shuttle Carrier Aircraft).

1:72-scale kits of the Orbiter have been made by both Revell and Monogram, which were different as they were then separate companies. More recently 4-D makes a 'visible' 1:72-scale Orbiter. Monogram also makes a full stack 1:72 Shuttle – it is likely that this is the largest commercial 'space kit' ever made, or ever likely to be made.

Tamiya made an Orbiter in 1:100, but there was no matching Booster section. In smaller scales

Revell 1:48-scale Apollo Spacecraft – 25th anniversary issue.

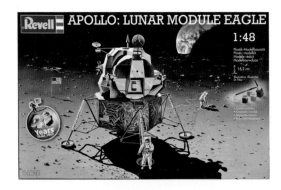

Revell 1:48-scale Apollo Lunar Module – 40th anniversary issue.

Monogram 1:32-scale Apollo Command-Service Module – one of a number of issues.

Airfix 1:72-scale Apollo Lunar Module – the most recent issue.

Monogram 1:48-scale Apollo Lunar Module – one of a number of issues.

The X-15

The X-15 is available as a true 1:72-scale kit from Monogram and MPM. The oft-quoted '1:72' Revell kit that dates as far back as 1958 is not, in fact, 1:72, but 1:65 – close, but not 1:72. However, recently the original Monogram kit has moved under the Revell name, so care must be taken to ensure that you have the '1:72'-scale kit and not the older 1:65. There are other scales of the X-15, but the conversion included here relies on a similar scaled XB-70, and for that there is really only one kit, the AMT version. (This is now under the Italeri name, but it is the same kit.) There are 1:48-scale X-15 kits, even one in 1:32, but a similar scale XB-70 would be impressive, though extremely impractical.

Monogram 1:72 North American X-15 – one of the two original boxes.

MPM 1:72-scale North American X-15.

AMT 1:72-scale North American XB-70 Valkyrie –
limited edition box.

Revell 1:48-scale Mercury and Gemini – first box.

Revell 1:24-scale Gemini – one of several boxes.

Gemini

Most Gemini conversions will use one of the two scales made by Revell, namely 1:24 and 1:48. Other kits have been available: Imai, also issued by Bandai, made one in 1:28 scale and Dragon has one in 1:72. There have been several in resin in 1:32 scale, especially from Collect-Aire and Raccoon, but firstly these were produced in small numbers and are consequently rare and expensive (if they can be found at all), and although they could be used in conversions, here we stay with conventional styrene. There are other Gemini spacecraft models, but they are far smaller and will be the payload for a Gemini-Titan II launcher vehicle.

Mercury

The Revell 1:48-scale Gemini was made as a double kit with America's first craft to carry an astronaut, Mercury. Unfortunately Revell never made a 1:24-scale Mercury kit to match the 1:24-scale Gemini, only the 1:48 (and 1:110 scales to go with its two launch rockets). Different kits from Horizon Models and Dragon come in 1:72, with launch rockets, but they are really too small for the conversions here. There are some resin kits in 1:32 scale, similar to the 1:32 Gemini, and there is one 1:24 scale from Sheri's Hot Rockets (and yes, 'Sheri' did exist!). It was designed to be launched on a flying model Mercury Redstone and was produced in injection styrene and resin, but is long out of production. Consequently the Mercury spacecraft conversion here is really restricted to the MRC/Atomic City kit, which is in 1:12 scale.

Atomic City/MRC 1:12-scale Mercury.

MPC 1:100-scale Pilgrim Observer: the second box.

Others

The Heller 1:125-scale Ariane 4 launcher is useful as it provides booster rockets, used in several conversions, and the MPC futuristic Pilgrim Observer space station can also supply some parts.

Heller 1:125-scale Ariane 4 launcher.

MATERIALS

You will also see the name of 'EMA' mentioned through the chapters. EMA stands for Engineering Model Associates, an American company that makes injection-moulded parts originally intended for professional model makers building models of industrial complexes, such as power stations, chemical plants and the like. These parts were soon discovered by the special effects industry (including this author), as they were ideal raw materials for building special effects miniatures and props.

Unfortunately for the general model maker, as a result of the growth of CAD-CAM, 3D printing and CGI for both the commercial model maker and special effects industries, the use of EMA parts has reduced, and these days many parts are difficult to obtain. However, EMA did branch out and start a 'hobby modeller' division, called Plastruct. This used the smallest scales of EMA parts, and introduced new shapes and sizes, primarily as tubes, rods and 'girder' shapes – I beams, T beams, L beams and the like. These can usually be found displayed in their own special rotating display on the counters of many model shops, or they are available online.

A very small selection of EMA parts with various catalogues.

Spare parts can be kept in their own kit boxes, large card boxes and specialist card storage trays.

MEASUREMENTS AND SCALES

'EMA' also brings in units of measurement, and how they are used throughout the book. The world works almost entirely in metric as the vast majority of countries use the metric system. However, the modern commercial model kit industry started – or at least was vastly expanded upon – in the UK and the USA. As both at that point used the British imperial system of measurements (and America still mainly does), the model kit industry followed suit. Hence the vast majority of scales are based on imperial units – so 1:72 and 1:48 scale for aircraft, 1:32 and 1:24 for cars, and

Plastic sheet, including plain and embossed.

1:144 for space rockets. This applies even with the model companies based in 'metric' countries, which also predominantly follow these scales.

Imperial measurement especially applies to EMA as it is an American company, so all its sizing is listed in inches and feet. To EMA its 6in-diameter tube is just that – 6in – and it has the code VT600. In many countries, however, it will be listed as the somewhat ungainly '152mm'. As EMA parts come into many of the builds in this book, the imperial measurement will come first in inches, followed, if necessary, with the equivalent in millimetres.

'Plastic sheet' will also be mentioned throughout the book. As its name implies, these are flat sheets of 'stock' polystyrene, usually in white (though black and other colours are made). It is made in various thicknesses, from 0.5mm up to several millimetres. Most hobby stores will sell it in small sheets, usually 8 × 12in, which is convenient, but expensive. Commercial plastic suppliers will usually have similar sheets in much larger sizes, such as 4 × 6ft, which, if you can source them (and transport and store them!), will be much cheaper. Cutting them down to working sizes requires a straight-edge and a suitable cutting tool.

However, note that a standard 'sharp-edged blade' is not really suitable for these sheets, nor for cutting styrene sheet in general. Special cutting knives/ blades are made that have a V-shaped edge that scores the styrene, allowing it to be 'snapped'. Model stores should have such knives, and they are available as extra blades for many 'Stanley'-type knives.

Plastic sheets are also available 'embossed' with patterns to reproduce 'full size' objects. Perhaps 'bricks' are the best known example here, though probably not much use for models of spacecraft (even for the 'tiles' on the Space Shuttle Orbiter!). However, other patterns include corrugated, and this can be useful for rolls around rocket sections – as seen, for example, on the Saturn V.

Other than that, most modellers, especially those who have been working at it for some years, will have acquired a well-stocked spares box, otherwise known colloquially as the 'bits and pieces' box (or more likely 'boxes'). These will – should – have all those, well, 'bits and pieces' that you will invariably find useful with such conversions as are found within these pages. You will be constantly diving down into them and rummaging around in them, and emerging with that small part and the exclamation 'Yes, that will do nicely…'.

TOOLS, PAINT AND CEMENT

If you are contemplating any of the builds in this book, you will almost certainly have a well-stocked model toolbox, with knives, files, sanding materials, clamps, modelling saws and hand-held 'pin-vice' drills, maybe even a small electric drill.

'Plastic cement', the type that came in tubes, is still available, and can still be used for standard 'plastic kits' moulded in polystyrene. However, most plastic gluing these days is of the liquid variety, based around some hydrocarbon solvent. Most of these are unpleasant to inhale, if not actually poisonous, so the advice is always to work in well-ventilated surroundings, and if you are particularly worried, to use suitable masks. Most liquid cements will glue polystyrene, but they will also glue other plastics, such as ABS (acrylonitrile butadiene styrene). As most of the EMA parts mentioned throughout this book are moulded in ABS, this is the only way to glue them.

Superglue – the common name for cyano-acrylate, or CA – is also very useful these days as it will glue – virtually – anything to anything else. With many kits being multi-material (that is, they are built up from more than one type of material) and with a predominantly polystyrene kit – with parts that can be resin, photo-etched and white metal, let alone any other materials you add yourself – superglue is indispensable. Sometimes even contact adhesive will have its uses, and spray glue in an aerosol is vital for

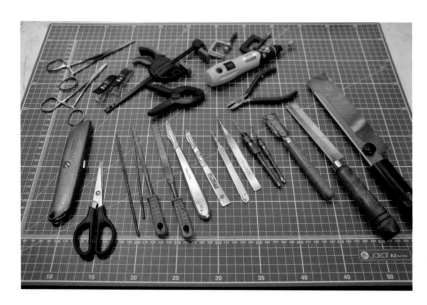

A selection of modelling tools, including knives, scalpels, files, saws and clamps.

A selection of modelling glues, decal softener, fillers and – old – brushes used for applying them.

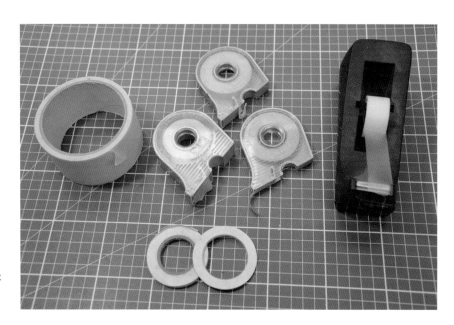

A selection of masking tapes – general masking (left); standard adhesive tape (right); and specialist model masking tape (centre).

applying gold foil, as again will be found throughout this book.

Paints used for model making have also changed, especially over recent years. Originally virtually all paints made for model makers were enamel based. This applied to both those in bottles or tinlets, and to spray paints. However, the vast majority of paints for modellers – and spray paint especially – have been reformulated to acrylics. This also applies to brush-on paints, though some companies, and in particular Humbrol, still make their traditional enamel paints in their traditional tinlets, supplemented by a similar range that is indeed acrylic.

CHAPTER 1

THE MERCURY OBSERVATORY

The Mercury capsule was small, with a maximum weight in space of around 3,000lb (1,376kg). It had an attitude control system enabling manual or automated controls to point it in a desired orientation, essentially rotating around its roll, pitch and yaw axes. Built by McDonnell, and wanting to see further development and more orders for its little Mercury capsule, the company funded a wide range of proposals for other uses.

Little was known about the space environment, but one problem that troubled NASA was the destructive effect of tiny micrometeoroid particles.

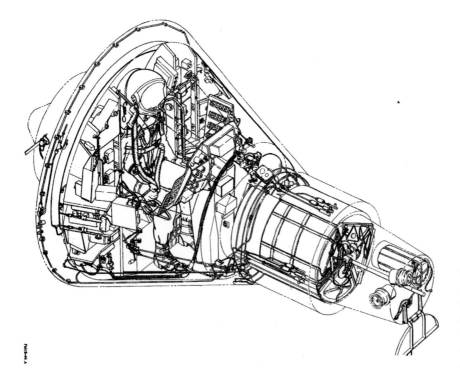

The tiny Mercury capsule was NASA's first major project, with several possibilities beyond its limited role carrying America's first astronauts.

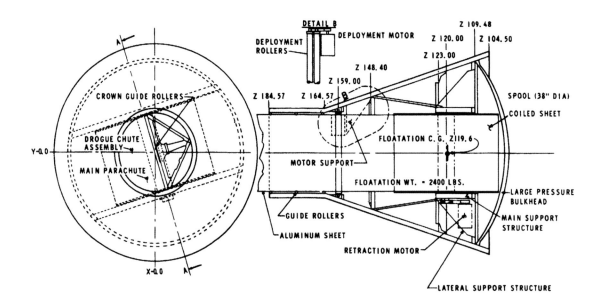

DETAIL B
DEPLOYMENT ROLLERS
DEPLOYMENT MOTOR
DEPLOYMENT MOTOR

Z 109. 48
Z 120. 00
Z 104. 50
Z 123. 00
Z 148. 40
Z 159. 00
Z 184. 57
Z 164. 57

CROWN GUIDE ROLLERS

SPOOL (38" DIA)

COILED SHEET

DROGUE CHUTE ASSEMBLY

FLOATATION C. G. Z119. 6

Y-0.0

MAIN PARACHUTE

MOTOR SUPPORT

FLOATATION WT. = 2400 LBS.

LARGE PRESSURE BULKHEAD

GUIDE ROLLERS

MAIN SUPPORT STRUCTURE

ALUMINUM SHEET

RETRACTION MOTOR

X-0.0

LATERAL SUPPORT STRUCTURE

The proposed layout for collecting micrometeoroid impact data involved rolled-out sheets of material to register hits.

With the potential risk to human life should the walls of a pressurised spacecraft be punctured, these threats had to be measured and quantified.

To get this information, one proposal was to equip an unmanned Mercury capsule with rolls of aluminium-covered Mylar that would unfold in space and test its suitability for protecting future manned vehicles. The ultra-thin aluminium foil would act as a recuperable capacitance gauge when connected to the terminals of on-board batteries, providing information through the electrical current about the size of impacting micrometeoroids and their frequency, together with the ability of the coated Mylar to resist being fractured by the collisions.

Another potentially more attractive application emerged after astronaut Gordon Cooper enthused over detail he could see from space on the surface of the Earth during his 22-orbit mission in May 1963. That year, the Central Intelligence Agency (CIA) and the National Reconnaissance Office (NRO) were already working on highly complex spy satellites for broad area surveillance and close-look reconnaissance.

McDonnell saw a potential application for an unmanned Mercury variant outside the range of non-military programmes. They approached the Air Force to propose the use of an unmanned Mercury capsule suitably modified for high-resolution imaging from space. Support came from specialist consultants, but having examined the capabilities of the Mercury spacecraft, the Air Force concluded that the limited weight-carrying capacity was too small for the kind of optical devices required for an orbital spy satellite.

Recoverable spacecraft were in their infancy, and Mercury was a ready-built solution to the problem of expensive equipment launched once and left in orbit. It was this potential for recoverability that championed the use of the Mercury spacecraft and offered a production-line vehicle to do that for a variety of applications.

It appeared logical on paper, but there were drawbacks with using the Mercury capsule. Electrical

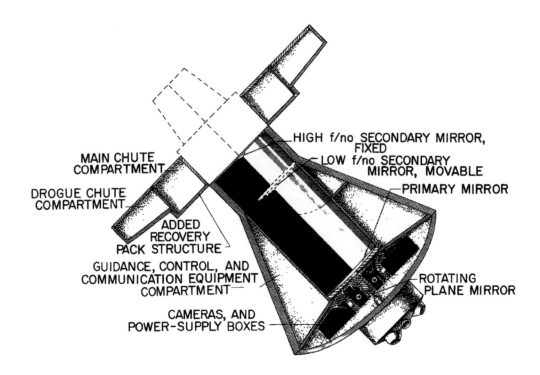

MAIN CHUTE COMPARTMENT

DROGUE CHUTE COMPARTMENT

ADDED RECOVERY PACK STRUCTURE

GUIDANCE, CONTROL, AND COMMUNICATION EQUIPMENT COMPARTMENT

CAMERAS, AND POWER-SUPPLY BOXES

HIGH f/no SECONDARY MIRROR, FIXED

LOW f/no SECONDARY MIRROR, MOVABLE

PRIMARY MIRROR

ROTATING PLANE MIRROR

Put together as an orbiting astronomical observatory, this unmanned version of Mercury was outcompeted by more sophisticated designs.

power was stored in batteries, and in Mercury there was no way of producing power from solar cells or small nuclear isotope generators. It would have negated the advantages in using an existing spacecraft if that had to be built. This meant that the operating life of a Mercury capsule was only a few days at most, and many of the potential applications proposed would have used large amounts of power, further reducing its operating life.

Nevertheless, the potential in Mercury's ability to return expensive pieces of equipment such as telescopic lenses, complex photographic instrumentation and even rolls of high-grade film for immediate processing, was attractive. McDonnell saw potential in fitting whole camera systems inside a Mercury capsule, and worked on a proposed observatory in space. The desire to place a telescope above the atmosphere predated the space age, and in 1964

NASA's Langley Research Center carried out a study to see whether Mercury could be adapted for this purpose.

All the internal life-support equipment would have been removed and replaced with this telescope, while the upper section of the spacecraft, which on a manned mission carried the forward recovery section, would be replaced with the optical tube, bringing light down the telescope to the camera. A separate toroidal recovery section would replace the original, with a parachute housing to either side of the forward section. To achieve all the desired advantages, Mercury's attitude-control equipment would be replaced with an equivalent, but much more accurate, stabilisation platform to achieve a pointing accuracy of 0.08 arc-sec during film exposure, which could last from seconds to several hours.

MODELLING THE MERCURY OBSERVATORY

If there is one thing optical astronomers hate, it's the Earth's atmosphere. To the human eye the sky looks clear, but viewing the skies through an optical telescope is invariably likened to viewing it from the bottom of a pond. To most astronomical instruments the Earth's atmosphere appears just as wavy and distorted as would the view to the human eye peering upwards through the water in the pond.

Here, sheet styrene plastic is cut (it is going to be thin, so scissors will probably be adequate) and glued into place. Odd gaps can be filled in with model putty and sanded smooth, but the general idea is that the UNITED STATES decal will eventually be applied over the top, so will hide any imperfections.

The Atomic City/MRC 1:12-scale Mercury spacecraft as used in this build. The main parts to be used are on the left and are black, except the hatch, which is supplied on the red runner – though this will end up black.

The hatch will be filled in place, but the window also needed filling in. The kit supplies the window in clear, and this can be used as a template.

Consequently, when space satellites became a reality, the idea of placing a telescope in orbit above the atmosphere must have been on the minds of many scientists and space engineers.

And given that the USA had launched a successful series of crewed spacecraft with one person on board – Project Mercury – it wasn't long before the idea of replacing the astronaut with a telescope came into being – hence this conversion. In effect this is a very early design for the Hubble Space Telescope, using the Mercury craft as the container for a reflecting telescope with a 30in (760mm) diameter mirror.

The basis for this conversion is the Atomic City/ MRC kit of the Mercury spacecraft in 1:12 scale. Unfortunately, although Revell made a 1:24-scale Gemini, a scale that may perhaps have been a more logical starting point, it never made a similarly scaled Mercury. The only Mercury spacecraft that Revell made was a 1:48-scale double kit, with a matching Gemini. This could be used, but it would make a rather small final result. There have been 1:32-scale resin kits of Mercury from Racoon, CollectAire and Crows Nest, and there was actually

19

one 1:24. However, the last was intended as the payload for a flying 1:24-scale Mercury Redstone, made by Sheri's Hot Rockets. But that company is out of production, so here the Atomic City/MRC kit is really the only kit that can be used.

You only need the outer structure for this conversion, as the interior is now purely the Cassegrain reflecting telescope – all traces of the human crew have been removed.

The Mercury has a hatch without a window, so here it can be simply cemented in place. Because of the way the parts are positioned on their runners, the main spacecraft is moulded in black, while the hatch is on the red runner (with the Launch Escape System). But as it is usual to paint the whole model, this will be turned black, along with the rest of the craft.

The Window

Slightly more of a problem is the window, as the telescope would have no need for one in this position, and if this version had even been built, one assumes it would never have been fitted in the first place – this area would be the 'shingles', as used for the rest of the exterior. The ideal solution would be to use another kit and cut out an appropriate area, but this would be somewhat wasteful and, needless to say, expensive. Alternatively, a section of the exterior could be moulded and a recast cast and used as a replacement.

But, given that the interior in this version doesn't need to be pressurised, the window opening would probably simply have been covered, which was done here. The kit instructions supply a template to cut the outer window from the supplied sheet of acetate, so here it is purely used as a template to cut sheet styrene to fill the gap. A small amount of filler may be necessary to fill the odd gap, but that should be it. It is also helpful to apply the UNITED STATES decal in the kit, over this section, so that will help hide the irregularities.

The Nose Section

The nose section of the telemetry and parachute compartments of the original Mercury are now all reserved for the parachutes, two drogue and two main, and as this is now split into two halves, the

The 'nose' section of the Mercury. The parts for the nose were first cemented together, and then sawn down the centre. Both halves have their edges 'cleaned up' by using a sanding board – simply a sheet of sanding paper spray-glued to a sheet of plywood or MDF.

A selection of tubing that could be used as the telescope tube. On the left is a length of EMA tube; in the centre is a cut section of a Saturn V; on the right is a part of an old build, using more EMA tubing, with an 'end' in place. Note that the main Mercury spacecraft – far left – has the hatch in place, and the window is filled and sanded.

Filling the inner surfaces of the modified nose cone with sheet styrene. Here the hinges are made from EMA parts – these are number KBC-10, and are intended to join girders together for architecture models, but bent wire could be used, fixed into drilled holes.

Sorting out the telescope tube. A section from a Saturn V rocket was used. All the interior surfaces – including the spider – will be spray-painted matt black. The interior surfaces of all optical telescopes need to be as 'matt – or flat – black' as possible.

first task is to glue the two main parts together. Then when thoroughly dry, these combined parts are cut down the centre. It is easiest to use the vertical moulding on the lower section to cut along, continuing into the upper section, to get two (more or less) identical halves. There are no illustrations to show what the new 'inner panels' would be. One assumes they would be closed in to protect the 'chutes during manoeuvres, so embossed plastic sheet, with a ribbed pattern, was used to block off both the inner areas and the lower.

Assuming the model is being built with this section folded back to reveal the telescope tube, they need some method to hold them at 90 degrees from the main body. They could be hinged, and small hinges are available from hobby suppliers, but here it was felt that it would be more suitable to fix them in place, otherwise nothing of the interior can be seen. For this, small EMA parts, with the reference KBS-10 or KBC-10 (they are intended to join girders), were used. KBS-10 can be used 'as is', while KBC-10 needs one end cut off. Then the U-shaped section of either fits neatly over the top of the spacecraft body. Alternatively, thin wire, bent at 90 degrees, could be used, fitted into drilled holes.

Making the primary mirror. This is the top of a Saturn V S-IC stage tank, using the inside surface. The hole in the centre needs to be carefully drilled accurately in the centre. (This is where the light passes through, bounced off the secondary mirror, to instruments that would be located behind the main mirror.)

The Interior: 'All' Telescope

As far as the interior is concerned, this is 'all' telescope. This consists of three parts – the telescope tube, the primary mirror and the secondary mirror and spider. The last is positioned at the top of the tube, the 'spider' being the structure that holds this

The main components for the build, left to right: the Mercury spacecraft; the primary mirror; the telescope tube; the heat shield, with the mirror support in place; the spider, with the secondary mirror; and the two halves of the opening nose.

More components, and the completed retro-rocket pack – bottom right – which is the same as fitted to the craft with an astronaut.

Fitting the telescope tube in place, and fitting the tube – the grey object on the right – that will take the rod for the stand.

secondary mirror in place. From the information available, this does indicate that a 'second' secondary mirror is positioned further down the tubes, but details are sketchy, so this is omitted.

The tube could be sourced from a variety of places. It needs to be approximately 2¾in (70mm) in diameter, and EMA makes suitable tubes (VT-275), though these are increasingly difficult to get hold of, are not cheap, and have to be bought in 36in (90cm) lengths. But given that it is purely a tube,

maybe a card tube could be sourced, then lined with thin plastic sheet. Alternatively, a tube could be made from flat plastic, rolled into a tube shape and cemented at the edges.

However, and by coincidence, the 1:144-scale Saturn V kit's S-II stage is 2¾in (70mm) in diameter and an almost perfect fit; a section was found in the 'bits and pieces' box, and was used here. The Saturn V kit will also supply a 'mirror' using the 'inside' one of the tank tops. This should strictly speaking be a parabolic section, which the tank top isn't, but at the end of the tube, the wrong cross-section is hardly noticeable. This needs a hole approximately $^3/_8$in (10mm) drilled in the centre, as this is a Cassegrain set-up – the light enters the top opening, hits the primary mirror, is reflected back up the tube to the secondary mirror, is refocused and then sent back down to the primary, but this time through the hole in the centre. Behind, a variety of instruments do the 'viewing'. (As this viewing is not being done by a human eye, technically the set-up is a Schmitt camera, but the telescope itself is still a Cassegrain.)

The secondary mirror is only seen from the back, and because the Saturn V kit is already being cannibalised, the heat shield part from the Apollo Command Module (CM) was used. The spider was built from EMA/Plastruct 'T'-shaped girders, and four arms were made. Strictly speaking only three arms are required, but four are easier to align, and many spiders use four. The spider is fitted up inside the top of the tube, and the whole assembly painted matt black. You can ignore painting the secondary mirror silver as it cannot be seen. However, the primary mirror does need to be 'silvered', and here the options are to use one of the 'chrome' sprays available – which, given that they are an aerosol, are very effective. Alternatively, use a material such as bare-metal foil, originally intended to reproduce the chrome on model cars, but this needs to be carefully applied to avoid creases on the surface.

The Retro-Rocket Pack

The only other part of the original kit that is used is the retro-rocket pack at the rear. Here the kit's parts can be built 'as is', with the option of adding the heat-control stripes as decals to the whole assembly. These stripes were added to the orbital flights, as the craft was in space longer than for the two first sub-orbital hops. The illustrations do not show them, but the telescope would certainly be in orbit for much longer than any of the crewed flights, so you have the option of adding these stripes, or omitting them.

The Main Paint Colour

Finally, the main paint colour of the Mercury (and Gemini) craft was not the oft-quoted 'dark blue'. This concept almost certainly originates from early photographs, where the reflection of sky and ocean often tinted the images towards the blue end of the spectrum. Besides which, if the film was Ektachrome, this is also slightly 'blue biased'. The craft were actually black, and for this, a black ceramic paint was used over the corrugated shingles that made up the exterior. Consequently, prime the whole of the exterior (and we assume the 'inner' panels of the opening nose) matt black, finished with a satin black to give a slight sheen. There is an argument for a very light

Using the kit decals – here the UNITED STATES, applied over the filled-in window section. Note the decal solvents (right) MicroSet and MicroSol, which are used to help encourage decals to 'settle' correctly, especially over an irregular surface (here, of course, on the corrugations on the exterior of the Mercury). Note the colour-coded brushes to ensure you don't mix up the two 'Sol' and 'Set' liquids, as they are different compositions.

The completed Mercury telescope, compared with the original crewed Mercury spacecraft. (The red Launch Escape System tower is omitted here.)

mist coat of a metallic black, but this is optional. The only exceptions to the exterior are the heat shield and retro-pack. The retro-pack is metallic light grey/silver (with or without the black stripes), while the heat shield for orbital craft is a metallic bronze colour.

No exterior markings are shown, though it is safe to say that the 'UNITED STATES' and stars and

The completed Mercury telescope on the specially built stand. The rear retro pack is attached exactly as it was with the actual Mercury flights.

stripes as supplied on the decal sheet would be used. Because of the size of the model there are many other small decals supplied for the many other markings scattered round the exterior; these would also most certainly still be there on the version, so it is up to the modeller to decide which to use.

Displaying the Model

Finally, you need to display the model. It will, just about, sit vertically on its retro-pack, but this is somewhat unstable, so it is better placed on a stand. Here a hole was drilled at the heat-shield end of the main body at an angle, and a thin tube with an internal diameter of ¼in (6mm) glued inside. A round wood base was cut from MDF (medium-density fibreboard), and a ¼in-diameter metal rod glued in the centre. Finally, fit the completed model in place.

The Mercury telescope, looking down the telescope tube, showing the primary mirror and the spider that holds the secondary mirror.

CHAPTER 2

THE ORIGINAL APOLLO SPACECRAFT

During April and May 1960 a team at the Space Task Group from NASA's Langley Research Center developed guidelines for further study of an 'advanced manned space vehicle'. This laid out requirements that would be put to industry for proposals, from which a winner could be selected for detailed design and manufacture.

Called Apollo, it was expected to fulfil two objectives with a single spacecraft design: provide a small laboratory in orbit, and conduct a reconnaissance of the Moon. The orbiting laboratory would allow observations of the Earth's surface, and support a small astronomical telescope operated by the crew; the lunar reconnaissance mission would be conducted by a flight round the Moon and back, but with the provision for going into lunar orbit on a later flight.

NASA anticipated the first Earth orbiting flights to begin in early 1966, followed by the lunar reconnaissance and laboratory missions a year later. When John F. Kennedy became President on 20 January 1961 he refused to authorise funds for Apollo. But on 12 April 1961 the Russians sent Yuri Gagarin on a single orbit of the Earth, and everything changed.

The design North American had proposed involved a Command Module (CM) and an Equipment Storage Module (ESM), with a Lunar Landing Module (LLM) below carrying a rocket motor for slowing down to a landing on the Moon and legs for supporting it on the surface. The LLM would use a cryogenic propulsion system for maximum efficiency, and the crew would lift off back to Earth using a rocket motor at the base of the ESM, leaving the redundant LLM on the Moon. The ESM would also provide power and supplies necessary for supporting the entire mission until it was jettisoned shortly before re-entry on the way home. Only the CM would carry the crew back through the atmosphere.

Seizing the publicity advantage of building the vehicle that would put the first men on the Moon, North American was on a high of optimism and ran advertisements to capitalise on its coup. But it was short-lived. A direct flight would require a rocket so large that the von Braun design team felt that it could not be designed, developed and built by the end of the decade. And while it would use smaller Saturn rockets already on the drawing board, the sheer complexity of orbital assembly left a lot of uncertainty.

Ball Brothers, an aero-engineering company, produced a concept for Apollo that would include support for astronomical instruments.

An early conceptualisation of the Apollo spacecraft, with lunar landing stage.

By mid-1962 a highly efficient way of conducting the landing had been mooted: Lunar Orbit Rendezvous (LOR), in which Apollo would carry a second spacecraft to lunar orbit, from where it would carry two men down to the surface. Apollo itself would get no closer than circling the Moon waiting for the lander to return, at which point it would bring the crew home. Selected on 7 November 1962, LOR would call for a second spacecraft, initially called the lunar excursion module (LEM), but eventually with the word 'excursion' deleted.

After the Moon commitment, and especially so following the LOR decision, plans swung into high gear on priority requirements and the development schedule for the several new technologies required. These included the decision to use fuel cells for electrical production. It quickly became apparent that two sequential developments of the Apollo spacecraft would be required to phase the introduction of systems essential to the Moon landing missions.

Apollo Block I would be used for Earth orbiting tests of the spacecraft and its propulsion systems, and for rehearsing essential procedures such as spacewalking, celestial navigation, and flights of up to fourteen days. Block II would be the fully developed spacecraft with all the systems required for supporting rendezvous and docking, deep-space missions and lunar orbit operations.

By 1963 there were to have been six Apollo A flights on six Saturn I launch vehicles between March 1965 and June 1966. Overlapping with the last of the Saturn I flights, a further eight Earth-orbiting Apollo flights would have been launched by Saturn IB between May 1966 and February 1968, overlapping the gradual transition to the Saturn V, the definitive launch vehicle for Moon missions.

1. Command Module
2. Equipment Storage
3. Earth Storable
   Liquid Propellants
4. Abort and Lunar
   Takeoff Propulsion
5. Lunar Landing Module
6. Hydrogen Tank
7. Liquid Oxygen Tank
8. Lunar Landing Propulsion
9. Landing Gear

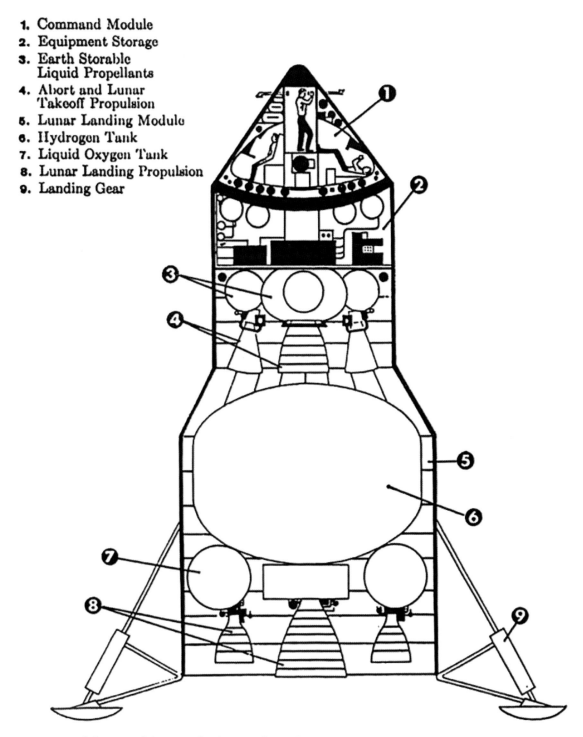

An annotated diagram of the moon-landing Apollo configuration, eventually rejected in favour of a separate lunar lander.

MODELLING AN ALTERNATIVE APOLLO

We are so used to seeing the classic Apollo space-craft set-up of Command Module, Service Module (SM) and Lunar Module (LM) that it is difficult to think that it could have been designed to work in a different way, and had come to look completely different.

With Project Apollo decided upon as the overall title of putting a 'Man on the Moon', the final result of LOR with a separate 'lunar lander', the LM, and a mothership, the Command Service Module (CSM), that remained in lunar orbit – was not in the plan at all. Instead most relied on a direct approach, where the whole craft travelled to the Moon, and made the landing. There were many proposed designs for this and they varied considerably – probably more than any other proposals in the chapters of this book.

Most did have some semblance of what ended up as the Apollo Command Module as the main

living compartment for the crew, although its size could vary, followed by the beginnings of the SM. However, the lunar landing part bore little, if any, resemblance to the final Grumman-built Apollo Lunar Module.

Even with these differences to the actual Apollo craft, here there were considerable variations. Some had the whole craft sleek and enclosed, rather in the manner of the 'Gemini-Apollo' – *see* Chapter 3 – while others only had the CM – or its equivalent – as an aerodynamic shape, as it would have to re-enter the Earth's atmosphere at some point. The rest was a cluster of modules, tanks and girder work that made even the actual LM look fairly restrained.

The build here ended up somewhat of a mix between the two extremes: it retains a 'standard' Apollo CM, part of a SM, and the landing section is based around the actual Apollo LM, although this does end up looking somewhat different. The basis used the ubiquitous Revell 1:48-scale Apollo Spacecraft kit that has been issued and reissued

The box for the first issue of the Revell 1:48-scale Apollo Spacecraft, from 1967. It is based on very early designs for Project Apollo, called 'boiler plates', and some details are wrong for the flight craft. However, even when built 'straight out of the box', the kit is still very impressive.

The History Makers' box for the Revell 1:48-scale Apollo Spacecraft, issued in 1983. Although the box-art is completely different to the first issue, showing a built model, the parts are identical to the first issue – and the several later issues for that matter.

many times, so should be easy to locate. This is also an ideal use of already built components that have seen better days but could be resurrected for this conversion, which is indeed the case here.

The Command Module

The crew section, the Apollo CM, varies in many of its concepts. In some it is actually smaller, carrying only two crew, while in others it could be larger, maybe up to four crew. But the overall shape and appearance looks the same as the actual Command Module, so an old one from the Revell 1:48-scale kit was located, and formed the starting point. The heat shield was already off, so the interior could be prised out for repair and repainting. However, even with the hatch open, very little can be seen and so it is sufficient just to paint everything inside a pale grey and either assemble it if it is a new kit, or, as in this case, to reassemble it. One thing to remember, however, is to remove the locating lugs for the LES (Launch Escape System), as this kit had the LES attached directly to the CM, whereas in actuality it attached to the BPC (Boost Protection Cover) that wasn't included in this original Revell kit.

The original kit also came with the semi-circular S-band antennae, which were not used on the flight-worthy CMs. However, they were already cemented

An already built Revell 1:48-scale Apollo service module that will form the basis for the new 'Ascent Stage' for this conversion...

... and an old Apollo Command Module from the same kit that was similarly sourced from the bits and pieces box, and the parts dismantled.

A selection of the parts that were selected for this build. In the end the SLA from the 1:48 Apollo kit (top left) was not used, nor the conical moulding (bottom right), but virtually everything else found its way into the build.

in place here, so were left. The only addition is a short ladder, which connects to the one that will run down the SM. The same type was used in the Gemini-Apollo conversion (*see* Chapter 3) from EMA/Plastruct, just to the right-hand side of the hatch, where the conduit that carried systems from SM to CM is located. The hatch itself was fixed in the open position.

The Ascent Stage

The Service Module depicted in many of the art works is much shorter than the actual SM, so here one that had already been assembled was cut approximately halfway along its length. In theory either 'half' could be used, but if you use the upper, it has the advantage of having the locating holes for the pins on the heat-shield of the CM, and the positions for the quad thrusters. The old lower bulkhead was refitted, though this was frankly to retain the integrity of the outer shell of the SM.

A smaller-scale Service Module, already built, from the Revell 1:96-scale version of the Apollo spacecraft, was found in the 'bits and pieces' box, and this formed the basis for the lower section of the new Ascent Stage. It is being test fitted against the upper surface of the original Apollo Lunar Module Descent Stage. The 1:48-scale service module that has already been cut down can be seen on the left.

Making the parts that will form the tanks for the new Ascent Stage. These are EMA parts, both 1in (13mm) diameter hemispheres (in green) and the grey 1in tubing. As these will eventually be covered in gold foil, what they are actually built from and what colour they are isn't important.

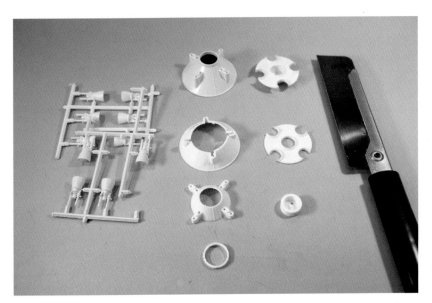

Cutting parts for the S-II engine stage of an Airfix Saturn V that will form the new landing rocket engines for the Descent Stage. The J-2 engine bells are on the left. Of the parts in the centre, the original kit part is at the top, while the next down shows the engine locator holes sawn away in the part's upper section – this is the part that will be used. The upper ring (bottom) is also cut away. On the right the central engine locator is cut from the surround, and this is glued into the sawn part next to it.

Some designs indicate external fuel tanks for this section – which in effect becomes the Ascent Stage for the whole craft. Consequently, some central column is needed that firstly attaches the 'shortened' SM to the lower Descent Stage, and secondly to hold these tanks.

A smaller SM from the 1:96 Revell Apollo kit (issued just as the Apollo Craft and also as part of the whole Saturn V) was located, again in the bits and pieces box, although a straight piece of tubing about 2in (50mm) in diameter could be used. The advantage of the Revell part is that it already has exterior detail on it, which saves adding features to a pristine new part.

The tanks for the new 'Ascent Stage' were made from EMA parts – tubing 1in (50mm) in diameter (VT-32), and hemispherical heads (that is, half spheres, HH-32); however, these will be finally covered in gold foil, so any suitable shapes – and they don't even have to be 1in – could be used. For example, ping-pong balls could be cut into halves, or even left 'as is' and instead make round tanks! The old Revell 1:96-scale SM was marked at 90 degrees around its circumference, and girder-work strips of plastic added, where the tanks will finally themselves be glued.

This new SM was primed and first painted semi-gloss white. Areas were then masked off on the upper, wider section that will remain white as a nod to the white radiator patterns on the actual Apollo SM. In actuality, the crewed Apollo Mission used Block II modules, where the white radiators were in a certain pattern. The earlier, uncrewed Apollo flights used Block I modules with a different white radiator pattern. However, the Revell 1:48-scale kit was produced so early on that the radiator pattern didn't even match a 'Block I' – it was a sort of 'Block 0'! However, here it doesn't matter – just choose a pattern that suits! Once masked, the whole ensemble is painted silver, and once dry, the masking is removed.

Two additions are required for the upper section. One is the quad thrusters, which can use the existing ones as used on the actual Apollo craft. If the top half of the original SM has been used, the quad positions are already there. If you have used the bottom half, they will have to be cemented to new locations.

One other part has to be added, which was not part of the original Apollo SM, and that is the access ladder. When we get to the new Descent Stage, the original Apollo method to reach the lunar surface has been used, so here a new ladder has to be added to reach the original LM platform (that was positioned outside the LM hatch). As with the Command Module ladder, EMA/Plastruct parts were used, with small L-shaped girder parts forming a method to raise the ladder slightly from the surface of the body of the SM.

The new tanks, covered with gold foil, are glued in place around the 'thinner' section of the new SM, and the gaps in between the tanks fitted with suitable-looking 'equipment'.

The source of gold foil has varied over the years. Originally the favourite supply was the thin gold foil found round many chocolate bars! But this then had to have a wrapper round it, creating two layers out of two dissimilar materials. More recently a plasticised material replaced these – usually polypropylene – which serves as both inner and outer wrapper, but unfortunately doesn't involve gold foil!

Some art and craft stores do stock similar types of material. And there is that old standby, kitchen aluminium foil; this has the great advantage that it is cheap and is available in large sheets, though its disadvantage is that compared to chocolate wrappers it is relatively thick, and only available in silver. But it can be spray-painted gold (or any other colour), and could be used if you can cope with its thicker nature. Any of these foils are best glued in place using one of the spray glues available from DIY and arts and crafts stores.

Regarding 'detailing parts', the Revell 1:24-scale Gemini kit has a wealth of suitable parts, supplied for its equipment module. Otherwise it is time to dive into that bits and pieces box. One item that can be fitted or omitted is the Ascent engine bell. If the plan is always to have the modules 'assembled', it can't be seen so might just as well be left out, and the Ascent Stage actually glued to the Descent. But if you want 'completeness', the existing Revell SM engine bell, even in 1:96 scale, is too large, so instead use the Ascent Stage engine bell that comes with the kit – though *see* the note in the next section regarding cutting a hole in the top of the Descent Stage.

The Descent Stage

Finally, the lower 'Descent Stage' must be assembled. Here the basis is the 1:48 Revell version, using the top and bottom plates and the side section. Note that the leg struts on the top plate where the legs attach need to be retained.

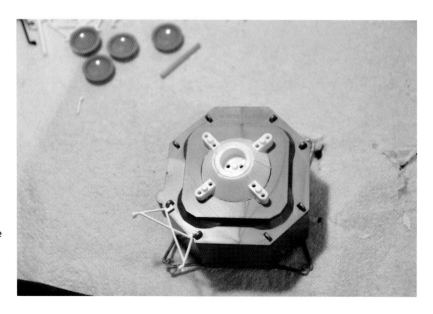

Cementing this new 'engine plate' to the underside of the original Revell Lunar Module Descent Stage. The cut part just covers the existing recess in the LM part.

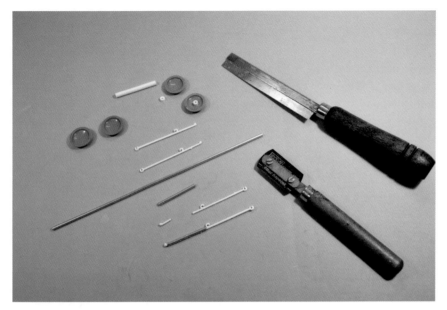

Extending the kit landing legs. *Top:* Although the existing LM pads could be used, here they were made larger by using EMA 'elliptical heads'. A locating socket was added from a short length of tube. *Below:* The existing kit landing legs were cut below the attachment point, and a length of aluminium tube superglued in place.

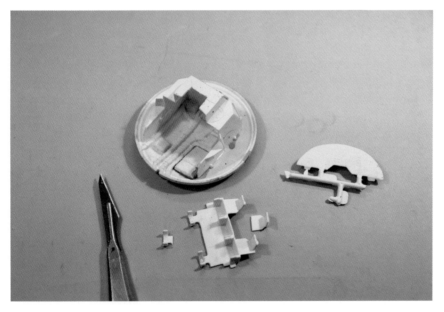

This craft would likely have carried only two astronauts, so the central couch position in the Command Module was removed. This is really a nicety, as once assembled, even with the hatch open, it can hardly be seen.

The newly built Ascent Stage also needs to be test fitted to the Descent Stage. A suitable locator for the new 'thinner' section of the SM (that is, the 1:96-scale SM) needs to be added to the top of the Descent Stage, in the form of a ring of plastic. In this case an EMA part (VX-200) 2in (5cm) in diameter was used, but it could be cut from a ring of thick plastic sheet. It will be covered in foil at a later stage, so the exact size and appearance is not critical.

If, as above, you want to fit an engine bell to the Ascent Stage, you will need to cut a hole in the upper

The component parts mostly built into their new configurations, but are not finished. The new Ascent Stage is at the back, with the Descent Stage (mostly in Apollo LM form) in front. There are four small tanks (for the Ascent Stage) in the centre (green and grey), while the two larger tanks, all grey, are centre left.

Spray glue is used to cement gold foil to the Ascent Stage tanks. A rough shape is cut out from the foil, the reverse (in this case the silver side) has a mist spray of the glue, and the foil is wrapped round the tank. Here the 'wrinkled' nature of the foil is intentional, so although you need to proceed with care, you don't have to be that precise! Any subsequent gaps can be covered over with more small scraps of foil.

plate, as the existing one is purely a shallow depression. Use the outline to aid the cutting, either with a very small saw, or literally drill holes all round the shallow edge, and snap the centre out and finish by using a half-round file and sanding to finish the cut edge. The interior of the Descent Stage could be furnished with tanks and other equipment, but these would hardly, if ever, be seen, so equally could be omitted.

As this new Descent Stage will be landing an upper section that is a lot heavier than the actual Apollo LM, illustrations show that more rocket engines are used. Here the engine plate from the S-II stage – the second stage of an Airfix 1:144-scale Saturn V – was used, glued in place directly over where the single engine bell from the kit would locate. The four outer engine locations are positioned so they line up with

The completed new Ascent Stage, apart from the quad thrusters and ladder. The four tanks are in place, and detailed parts added to the gaps in between.

the landing legs, but there is no reason why they cannot be rotated 45 degrees so they line up with the 'long sides' of the Descent Stage.

Raising the Landing Height

Because of these new engines, the landing height has to be raised, and the most straightforward method is to extend the main landing legs. For strength, small-diameter aluminium tube was used. The existing plastic legs are cut just above the pad locating pins (so retain their angle where they fit the holes in the pads), and the tubing runs right up to the first articulated join. The exact extended length is not critical – about 1in (25mm) will be sufficient. So the tubing will need to be $1/8$in (3mm) in diameter, and the old leg sections slid inside and superglued in place.

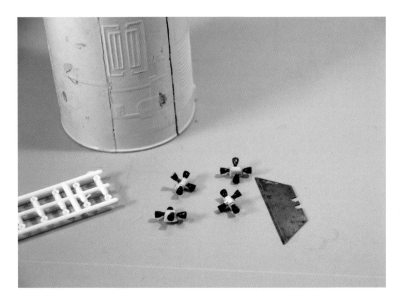

Assembling the quad thrusters for the Ascent Stage. These are the ones that are included in the Revell kit. Each nozzle is a separate part – some still on the runner on the left – and consequently vulnerable to being knocked off! To strengthen, drill a small hole in the nozzle and a corresponding hole in the quad body and glue in with superglue a very short length of metal rod.

Applying gold foil to the new Descent Stage, using an Apollo LM as a guide to match up the finish. The new Descent Stage has already been painted satin black, and silver foil applied to the upper surface.

The underside of the new Descent Stage, with the extended landing legs, and the very prominent five engines, instead of the actual Apollo LM's one. The two new tanks have also been covered in gold foil and glued to the main structure.

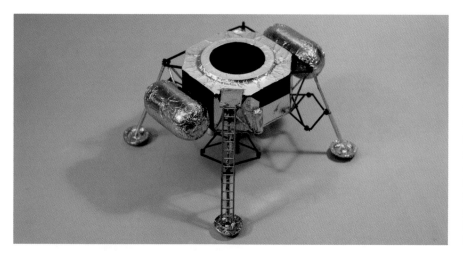

The new Descent Stage the right way up, with all the paint and foil in place. The original platform, outside the original hatch, is in place, with an extended Plastruct ladder as the legs are longer.

The completed Ascent and Descent Stages. Note the ladder now added to the outside of the Ascent Stage, which stretches down to the original platform from the original Lunar Module that is cemented in the same position.

The new Descent Stage design also has new fuel tanks (for all those extra engines) and here two were built, using larger diameter EMA tube and hemispherical ends – around 1¼in (32mm). However, they are again covered in gold foil, so even card tube and flat ends could work perfectly well.

Other than these additions, the rest of the original Descent Stage was finished much as it was for the actual missions. The sides were painted satin black, and gold foil used at the short sections where the legs are located. Silver and gold foil was used on the underside, while the upper surface used just silver. The landing legs were finished in satin black, silver foil and gold foil, and the pads themselves in gold. Much of it ended up matching what the actual Apollo LM looked like. A longer ladder is needed down the appropriate leg, and the existing small platform fitted in place; both are painted silver. The five engine bells (Saturn V, J-1 engines, as they fit the engine plate) are painted aluminium and glued in place.

Any markings, as with any build in this book, are speculative, and the ones that come with the Revell kit can be used, plus others that look right. The display could be alongside a 'real' Apollo LM, when the immense difference in height will be immediately apparent, or displayed on a base with the Apollo 11 equipment found in the Monogram Lunar Module kit (as with the Gemini-Apollo – *see* Chapter 3).

The new 'Alternative Apollo' next to an actual Apollo lunar module: this definitely shows off the difference in height.

The 'Alternative Apollo' on the base with the Apollo 11 astronauts and equipment, supplied in the Monogram Lunar Module kit.

TWO MEN TO THE MOON

On 25 May 1961 John F. Kennedy pledged to put astronauts on the Moon by the end of that decade. But original objectives for Apollo needed to be prac- tised long before it was ready to fly, if only to verify

design capabilities. In December 1961 NASA gave McDonnell Aircraft a contract for a two-man version of their Mercury capsule. Named Gemini, after the constellation with the two stars Castor and Pollux, it

The two-man Gemini spacecraft with the white adapter flared out to expand its diameter to that of the upper stage of the Titan launch vehicle, NASA's first multirole spacecraft.

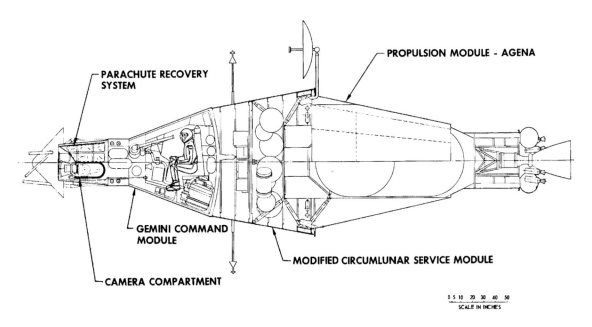

A circumlunar Gemini concept using a modified Agena stage.

was expected to begin operations in 1963 or 1964, demonstrating docking, space-walking and long duration flight.

McDonnell produced a report dated 10 April 1964 proposing a Gemini spacecraft launched to a circumlunar trajectory by Saturn IB with an Agena D or a Centaur upper stage. The ejection seats would be replaced by a Mercury/Apollo-style launch escape tower, and a greatly enlarged Equipment Module (EM) would carry additional hydrogen and oxygen tanks for the fuel cells. The heavy retro-rockets would not be required, and telephoto, mapping and panoramic cameras would be added to the nose of the spacecraft.

An optional alternative for a lunar orbit mission was also proposed, with twelve orbits over a 24-hour period in a path of 103 miles (166km) by 92 miles (148km), with an attached Agena for returning the spacecraft to Earth: this raised the total weight to 24,647lb (11,180kg). Orbital photo-reconnaissance would allow additional high-resolution stereo cameras to be carried, and a wide-field mapping camera for studying the topography. The orbital inclination would have been 14.5 degrees to the Moon's equator, and take in a wide range of sites that were, even in 1964, on the shortlist for manned Moon missions.

McDonnell had been fixated on Gemini lunar missions since mid-1961. Called the *Direct Flight Apollo Study* and dated 31 October 1962, McDonnell described how NASA could get two men on the lunar surface using an existing spacecraft already in detailed design. The report was compiled just as NASA was making the decision to adopt the LOR (Lunar Orbiting Rendezvous) mode, and McDonnell adopted the Saturn V as the launch vehicle for its lunar Gemini. Saturn V had a capability of sending 90,000lb (45,360kg) to the Moon.

It failed to convince managers, but McDonnell did come back with a lunar rescue plan, offering NASA the opportunity to invest in the essential elements of that concept, and apply it to a back-up in case the Apollo Lunar Module (LM) was stranded on the surface, or if the main Apollo Command Service Module (CSM) was unable to get out of lunar orbit. But there was insufficient money for that

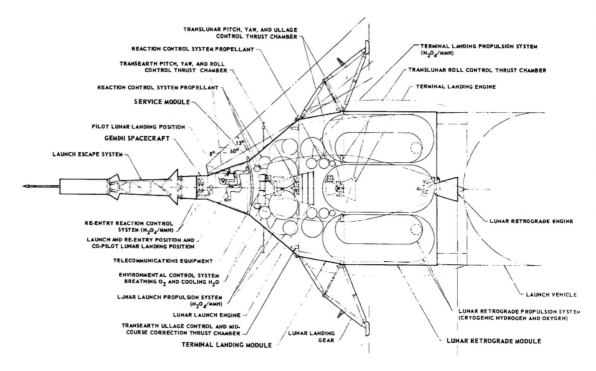

TRANSLUNAR PITCH, YAW, AND ULLAGE
CONTROL THRUST CHAMBER

REACTION CONTROL SYSTEM PROPELLANT

TRANSEARTH PITCH, YAW, AND ROLL
CONTROL THRUST CHAMBER

REACTION CONTROL SYSTEM PROPELLANT

SERVICE MODULE

PILOT LUNAR LANDING POSITION

GEMINI SPACECRAFT

LAUNCH ESCAPE SYSTEM

RE-ENTRY REACTION CONTROL
SYSTEM (N_2O_4/MMH)

LAUNCH AND RE-ENTRY POSITION AND
CO-PILOT LUNAR LANDING POSITION

TELECOMMUNICATIONS EQUIPMENT

ENVIRONMENTAL CONTROL SYSTEM
BREATHING O_2 AND COOLING H_2O

LUNAR LAUNCH PROPULSION SYSTEM
(N_2O_4/MMH)

LUNAR LAUNCH ENGINE

TRANSEARTH ULLAGE CONTROL AND MID-
COURSE CORRECTION THRUST CHAMBER

TERMINAL LANDING MODULE

LUNAR LANDING
GEAR

TERMINAL LANDING PROPULSION SYSTEM
(N_2O_4/MMH)

TRANSLUNAR ROLL CONTROL THRUST CHAMBER

TERMINAL LANDING ENGINE

LUNAR RETROGRADE ENGINE

LAUNCH VEHICLE

LUNAR RETROGRADE PROPULSION SYSTEM
(CRYOGENIC HYDROGEN AND OXYGEN)

LUNAR RETROGRADE MODULE

The proposed Gemini lunar lander with the deceleration (retrograde) stage shown in this schematic.

contingency, although NASA would be haunted by the thought of such a fate until the very last flight.

After Apollo 13 and the analysis of risk and failure probability, NASA became increasingly concerned at the possibility of a total loss of vehicles and crew. It is also interesting to note that this fear permeated the White House. When in 1972 President Nixon approached elections for his second term in the White House, he demanded that the last Moon-landing attempt be postponed until after the votes had been cast – not wanting a catastrophe to compromise his chances! So Apollo 17 was delayed until 7 December, one month after the election.

Back in the mid-1960s, however, the US intelligence community was convinced that Russia would mount a manned circumlunar flight for the 50th anniversary of the October 1917 revolution. It was by no means certain that Apollo could conduct

such a flight by then. But McDonnell were determined to have an answer, and they came up with a proposed circumlunar Gemini programme from their lunar landing mission concept.

Known as Gemini L, it was presented to NASA in July 1965, at its own request calling for a modified Gemini A (Gemini B was related to a military potential) launched by Titan II into Earth's orbit to dock with a Transtage booster placed in orbit by a Titan IIIC. Weighing 8,800lb (3,990kg), Gemini A would dock to a standard docking adapter placed on one end of the Transtage, and its motor used to push the assembly, with a length of 36.7ft (11m), to a circumlunar trajectory and splashdown 72 hours after launch. An alternative concept called for the Gemini L spacecraft to be launched by Titan IIIC, or for two Transtage boosters docked in tandem to Gemini A.

MODELLING A 'GEMINI' APOLLO

We are so used to seeing the Apollo craft as the Command and Service Modules, and the spidery LM, that it is somewhat difficult to imagine them as different shapes and sizes, but that would have happened if one proposal for a different type of 'Apollo' had occurred, as this would have used an existing Gemini craft, not a newly built spacecraft. Confusingly, it would still be termed 'Project Apollo', just not using an 'Apollo' spacecraft!

Quite a few drawings and artwork exist for what could have been a 'Gemini spacecraft-based Project Apollo'. They all differ in detail, of course, but they all show a three-stage craft, with a Gemini spacecraft perched on top of what would be the Ascent Stage of this new design, itself on top of the Descent Stage. The names of the 'Ascent' and 'Descent' stages may be borrowed from actual Apollo terminology, but that's about where the commonality ends, as these designs show the whole three-stage craft on the lunar surface, not as the actual case of the flown Apollo when only the two-stage LM

The two main kits used in the conversion, both from Revell. The whole Apollo spacecraft is in 1:48 scale. Although based on very early plans, this is still an impressive kit and has been issued a number of times, both by Revell Inc in the USA and Revell-Germany for Europe. The Gemini spacecraft comes from the Revell Mercury Gemini double kit, also in 1:48 scale. This has also been issued a number of times, including under the Monogram name. The box shown here is an original issue.

performs the actual landing (using LOR, where the main crewed ship – that is, the CM – stays in lunar orbit).

As in all the examples in this book, any details that are available vary quite considerably, but one commonality is that the two landing stages – Descent and Ascent – would be cone shaped, totally unlike an Apollo LM. However, the Descent Stage was shown having landing legs similar to those that were eventually used on the Apollo LM. The Ascent Stage was purely a cone shape, and the existing Gemini craft perched on top at the very apex.

What was slightly alarming was that the two astronauts would have to use a very long ladder to reach the surface of the Moon. Actually there were three ladders, split between the Gemini itself, then down the Ascent Stage, and because the Ascent and Descent Stage cones were at different angles, there was a third to reach the surface. The actual one-section ladder of the Apollo LM pales into insignificance by comparison, and although the crew would be assisted in that the climb down – and up – by being in $^1/_6$th G, this would still have been fairly daunting, and could have been the main reason why this approach was not followed up.

The Build

Creating such a model of a Gemini Apollo starts with the question 'in what scale?' There are only two generally available model kits of Gemini craft, both Revell, one in 1:48 scale, the other twice the size, in 1:24, which somewhat limits the choice. The 1:24 kit would be interesting, but would end up with a finished result that was over 16in (400mm) high and over 18in (460mm) across the landing legs. It would be nice, but would need some display space. A 1:48-scale Revell Gemini was therefore used as the starting point.

Both Revell kits of Gemini were based on early plans for the craft, and both feature the indentations in the outer shell, in front of the doors, which is wrong. In the final flown craft this area followed the curvature of the outer casing. However, this is 'fictional', so unless you feel so inclined to convert the kit parts, use it 'as is'.

The Gemini is built straight from the kit; the only really visible addition is the topmost part of the descent ladder, but that will be dealt with when we come to 'ladders' in general.

Building the Ascent and Descent Stages

There is no real option when it comes to building the Ascent and Descent Stages except to create them from scratch. However, the Revell 1:48 Apollo Craft kit is a good starting point, for the Descent Stage especially. This was built from the lowermost section of the SLA (the Spacecraft Lunar Module Adaptor; where the LM was housed for actual Apollo missions). This was shortened by about ¾in (20mm), so ended up about 2in (50mm) in height.

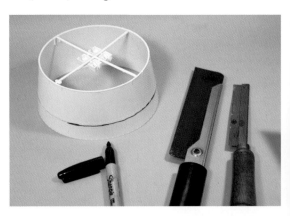

Shortening the lower section of the Apollo SLA to create the 'Descent Stage' for the conversion. It is marked with a felt-tipped pen and will be cut with a razor saw. Two sizes of saw are shown here.

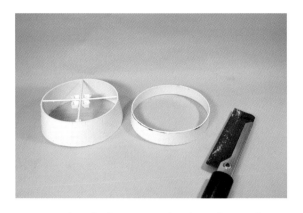

Removing the bottom section from the Apollo SLA, using a razor saw. This unwanted section is approximately ¾in (2cm) in height. At this stage the cross-shaped runner at the top of the part – seen on the left – has been left on, as it gives some rigidity for handling.

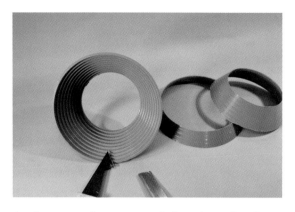

Sorting out various EMA conical sections. This shows the inner surface with its indentations, useful for cutting these cones to size. Run a sharp blade or a specialist cutting tool (shown) round the inside, and the section will snap away reasonably easily.

The rigidity of the modified SLA is useful when sanding the lower edge smooth, using a sheet of sanding paper spray-glued to a piece of plywood.

Collecting the three basic section shapes together. *Left*, the stock Revell 1:48-scale Gemini spacecraft; *centre*, the Ascent Stage, based on an EMA 60-degree cone; *right*, the Descent Stage, based on the Revell 1:48-scale SLA, cut down to 2in (50mm) in height.

The Ascent Stage

The Ascent Stage cone is the most difficult to source. Here, this ended up as an EMA 90-degree cone, part number VC-90, the lower section of which needs matching to the upper diameter of the Descent Stage cone, and the upper section cut to match the diameter of the Gemini heat shield. EMA cones have indentations inside that allow for easier cutting down to smaller sizes.

EMA cones are not cheap and not generally available (*see* the Introduction for explanations, and the Appendix for addresses and suppliers), and a similar shape could be cut from plastic sheet, curved round to make the cone shape. The two joining edges could be overlapped and cemented, or joined with plastic strip. As these are 'fictional' designs, details such as where a join line is, and what forms the join, are not important, and such 'join connections' might just as well add to the overall detailing.

Once the two cone shapes have been decided on (however they are made), both need additional work. There are two options. First, the Ascent Stage could be purely cemented to the Descent, so in fact does not need any internal detailing. However, if you do decide to go down this route, you are free to decide how much – or how little – detailing goes into this section. Obviously an Ascent engine (as per the Apollo Lunar Module) would be needed, but everything is very much up to the builder.

The three sections test-fitted together.

If you wish to furnish the interior of the Ascent Stage, here trial fittings are shown with the central section of an Airfix Saturn V, an S-IC engine bulkhead with its central F-1 engine, surrounded by various parts from Revell's 1:24-scale Gemini equipment module.

Whether an interior of the Ascent Stage is fitted out or not, externally the various thrusters' panels will be required. This is especially to hold the Gemini spacecraft securely at the apex. Tags on its heatshield fit in slots in these parts, seen still on their runner on the left.

One way would be to cut circles of plastic sheet to fit inside the EMA cone, using a pair of compasses, fitted with a cutting blade – very useful for this type of work. The engine plate could come from a Saturn V S-IC first stage, and one of the five F1 engines used here, as this rocket motor. Around could be scattered some of the components from the Revell 1:24-scale Gemini, the equipment section of which has a very useful selection of tanks of various sizes and other useful pieces of equipment. But, as indicated, this section can be omitted, and the Ascent Stage never removed from the Descent.

The Descent Stage

The Descent Stage does have to have additional detailing, as it needs the landing legs at the very least, and it was decided to adapt the Revell 1:48-scale Lunar Module parts to this conversion. Here, the legs are quite a bit further apart than for the Apollo LM, so the top of the LM Descent Stage was cut to separate the four landing-leg supports. These were then marked on the cone where the struts will fit. The kit part of the SLA cone has the attachment points for the opening

Cutting circles in plastic sheet is made considerably easier with one of these special compasses (centre) in yellow plastic. These can be fitted with a sharp cutting blade. Drill a very small hole in what will be the centre of the final disc to take the centrepin of the compasses. Set the compasses to the correct radius and swing round the centre, using the blade to score the plastic sheet. You don't need to cut through completely, just score enough so the plastic sheet will snap away.

Using the top of the Revell 1:48-scale lunar module Descent Stage as the basis for the conversion. The outer section, with the leg attachment points, needs separating away from the centre, glued into the slot in the edges of the SLA section, and the five pieces joined up with scrap plastic sheet. The disc at upper left – cut with the compasses as before – is then cemented over the lot to strengthen and give a flat surface.

panels of the SLA, which are convenient points to fit these parts – they are already equally spaced at 90 degrees around the cone, so don't need any further measurement.

The centre of the original Revell part is also used, and as these five parts are now separated and spaced out, strengthening plastic strips were added to join them. Another circle of plastic was then cut out, with a suitable hole in the centre, and cemented on top, to strengthen the whole assembly.

A disc of plastic is also cut out for the underside of this Descent Stage, but fitted about ¼in (6mm) below the bottom edge. The bottom part of the Apollo LM is also used, but the centre section (with the hole for the engine well) is cut away from the surrounding, and cemented directly in the centre of this new disc. The engine bell from the kit can be used, but is best glued in position later.

The outer sections of this lower plate of the LM are also needed, as these have the bottom part of the original Apollo LM that is also used, with the U-shaped connectors that hold the landing-leg mechanism. These need separating from their surrounds and are used upside-down compared to their Apollo LM orientation, though they will end up doing the same job. Mark in line with the upper struts, and cement these separate parts in line. Cutting into the lower edge of the Descent Stage will help to locate them. They are then cemented (remember, upside-down!) to the lower edges of this new Descent Stage, directly below the upper struts; the precise fitting, regarding smooth surfaces, isn't too important as they will eventually be covered with foil.

The LM legs from the original kit are used intact. The only slight difference is that the ladder is not used, and the extended mechanism is not extended out flat, as it doesn't leave enough space between the engine bell and the surface. An alternative would be to make extended legs to get round this problem, but we are back to 'what ifs', so exact details do not matter too much.

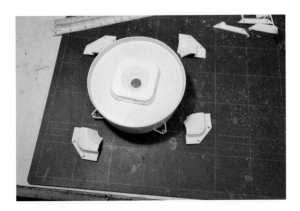

The Ascent Stage turned upside-down. First the original Revell Apollo LM Descent Stage engine plate is cut away and glued into the centre of a disc, cut by the methods described previously. But retain the outer sections.

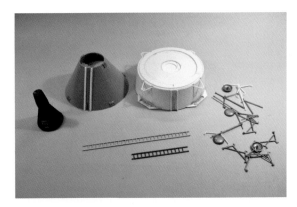

The three main assemblies before painting and detailing: *left*, the stock Revell 1:48 Gemini spacecraft; *centre left*, the Ascent Stage, with the ladder supports (the white strips) in place; *centre right*, the Descent Stage; *right*, the stock lunar module landing legs from the Revell kit. *Below centre*, two of the three ladders cut from EMA/Plastruct parts (the one for the Gemini is not shown here).

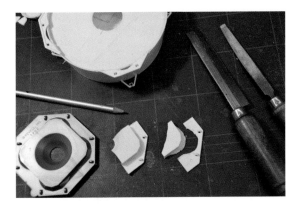

The outer sections of the Revell lunar module base (lower centre). The raised area is then trimmed away (lower right), and this 'C'-shaped part cemented upside-down to the bottom edge of the new Descent Stage (upper centre). An intact lower plate from the kit is shown at bottom left.

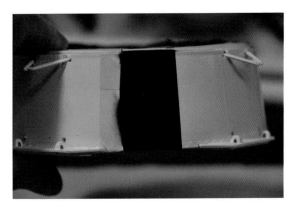

The main Descent Stage has been sprayed gloss white, and masked so some areas can be sprayed satin black. Note the lower lugs for the landing legs in position on either side of the black panel. These are directly under the top supports as they are in the Apollo LM kit, but here they are fitted upside-down.

Building the Ladders

The last pieces of equipment that need building are the ladders. Many kits have ladders in them – for example, railway accessories kits have ladders to signal gantries and the like. Here, small EMA ladders

Exactly which parts to cover in foil, and which to paint black or silver, is arbitrary. Here a different pattern was used from that of an Apollo LM, just to ring the changes. The LM legs from the Monogram kit could be used instead, but these are better detailed than the Revell, and given that these are based on designs that never flew (let alone built), keeping it simple is frankly probably the better option.

were used, from its Plastruct division, parts number KL-8. These come in 12in (305mm) lengths, and one length was enough for all three. They need raising from the surfaces of the stage, and angled girders were used (more EMA/Plastruct parts) so the ladder fits inside the 'angle'. These supports were then glued to the Ascent and Descent Stages before painting.

A ladder is also needed for the Gemini craft, and this is slightly different from the other two. It is positioned in between the two opening doors, and the same ladder is used, but to fit, it has to be reduced in width as it reaches the upper parts of the craft, otherwise the hatches will not open! It is simplest to cut the rungs in the centres very carefully, and very gently push the sides together, then glue. The rungs are small and thin, so great care will be needed to ensure they don't snap.

The Finish

The various artworks of this design show that the likely finish would be that the Gemini craft itself remains in its existing 'black' finish, while the two new stages are

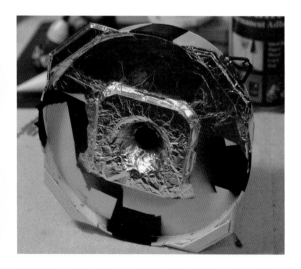

Working on the Descent Stage (centre) and applying both gold and silver foil to the underside. 'Old style' chocolate wrapper foil is used here, glued in place with spray glue, a can of which is shown upper right in the background.

either silver, maybe with black panels and stripes, or white, with black panels and gold foil. The Apollo LM was silver and black, and silver and gold foil, and variations on this finish were selected. But as before, the exact layout isn't perhaps the main point, and here we are really down to 'what looks good'!

The Descent Stage

The Descent Stage came first, as the positioning of its colour pattern dictates where the finish goes on the Ascent Stage. Consequently, it was primed and painted semi-gloss white, using Humbrol aerosol paints. Once thoroughly dry it was decided to paint the areas between the legs semi-gloss black.

The original SLA part that forms the main cone here is conveniently marked out with vertical lines, so it is easier to select those in the centre, mask each side with good quality modelling masking tape (Tamiya tape is recommended), then mask the rest of the structure. Cheaper tape can be used here, and even old polythene bags, salvaged from those in the kits that pack the parts. (These are good for recycling, even if in reality you've only recycled them this once, as after this they will really not be usable again.) One point to make is *do not* use ordinary paper for masking, as the paint will almost certainly seep through.

Once masked, the black paint can then be sprayed on, and once 'tacky' dry, the masking tape carefully removed. The reason for 'tacky dry' is so when the direct masking line – here between the black and the underlying white – is removed, the paint will 'flow' imperceptibly and will even out the different surface levels. (This process really *is* imperceptible, so don't worry too much about it! It comes more into play when you are masking high-gloss two-tone colours on, for example, model cars.)

The final finish here uses gold foil, as detailed in Chapter 2. Again this uses the fact that it can be applied as a crinkled surface, and is ideal for hiding a perhaps imperfect surface finish. It shouldn't really be relied on for this, but frankly this is a definite benefit on many occasions! Here for the Descent Stage, the engine bell mounting was covered in silver (as per

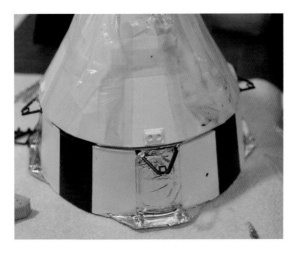

The Descent Stage with both paint and gold foil applied, and the Ascent Stage in position, so its black panels can be lined up to the Descent and masked off.

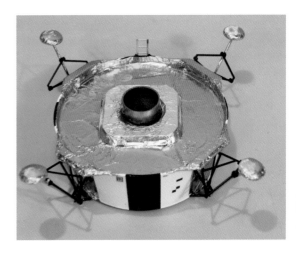

The completed Descent Stage, upside-down with the foil in place, and the landing legs. Note these are finished in a mix of silver and gold foil, as well as black and white paint.

the real Apollo LM) and – as the gold foil used here, turned over – the other side is silver. The remainder of this underside was then covered in gold foil.

Small sections of the gold were then cut and glued behind the areas where the legs attach. More was rolled round the legs and landing pads, and some areas were left black – though you could foil *all* the leg sections.

The Ascent Stage was then placed on top, rotated to line up the ladder positions. The areas above the

leg positions were masked off, approximately half-way up the sides, and spray-painted semi-gloss/satin black.

Gluing the Ladders and Applying the Decals

The final task is to glue the ladders, painted silver, in position, and decide if you want any markings on the finished model. The various kits used in this

The three completed modules – *left*, Gemini; *centre*, Ascent Stage; *right*, Descent Stage. (Note that the top of the Descent Stage isn't 'finished', as it is covered by the Ascent Stage.)

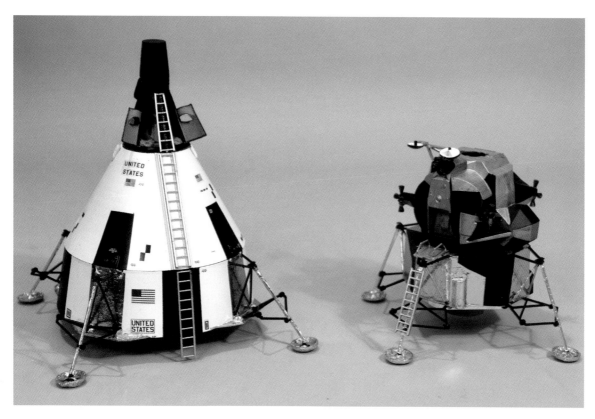

The complete and assembled 'Gemini' Apollo, compared with the actual Apollo LM – here the Revell kit, on which the new Descent Stage is based.

build have their own decals, so obvious ones, such as UNITED STATES and the US flag, were used here. Other decals can be found on specialist sheets. Block colours can be cut from stock decal sheets of one single colour. These could replace painting large areas if you want. Other sheets give stripes of various thicknesses and colours, so again can be used to create dividing lines.

Some of the smallest decal details do not have to be 'space' oriented as such. There are many decal sheets, both those found in kits and those from after-market suppliers, for aircraft that contain a multitude of small labels, circles, squares or panels, all of which could be put to good use.

Displaying the Model

One option is to stand the build alongside a similarly scaled Apollo LM for comparison. Examples in 1:48 are the original Revell, on which parts of this build were used, or the Monogram equivalent, or the newest, that from Dragon. The latter two are better detailed than the Revell, useful though that is, but the Revell was made very early on in the development of Project Apollo, and so lacks some of the final details.

Alternatively, mimic what Apollo did for real, and land your Gemini Apollo on the Moon, with two astronauts and all their equipment, using the Monogram part as in Chapter 2.

CHAPTER 4

AN AIR FORCE GEMINI

NASA opted for the two-man Gemini spacecraft as a bridge between the tiny, one-man Mercury capsule and the three-man Apollo spacecraft destined to put two men on the Moon by the end of the 1960s. NASA was not the only customer wanting to operate the two-man Gemini spacecraft, but it fought hard to keep control of Gemini, and it managed to.

In January 1963 the Department of Defense began its Manned Orbiting Laboratory (MOL), a cylindrical facility capable of conducting extensive reconnaissance

The two-man Gemini re-entry module would be the core for a wide range of applications for this durable but small spacecraft.

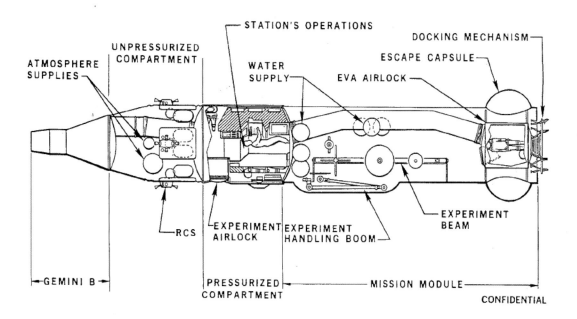

ATMOSPHERE SUPPLIES
UNPRESSURIZED COMPARTMENT
STATION'S OPERATIONS
WATER SUPPLY
EVA AIRLOCK
DOCKING MECHANISM
ESCAPE CAPSULE
RCS
EXPERIMENT AIRLOCK
EXPERIMENT HANDLING BOOM
EXPERIMENT BEAM
GEMINI B
PRESSURIZED COMPARTMENT
MISSION MODULE
CONFIDENTIAL

MOL would have been used as the basis for a wide range of applications, including this Double-MOL configuration as an experimental research facility.

and surveillance using high-powered telescopes with cameras, and for scientific research in orbit directly applicable to its mission goals. It would be supported by a Gemini that would carry the two crew home.

Designated Gemini B, the Air Force variant would be launched on top of MOL by a Titan heavy-lift launch vehicle, a development of the Titan II used to send NASA's Gemini capsules into orbit, but with large, strap-on, solid propellant boosters. Gemini B for MOL flights would remain docked to the laboratory until the time came to return to Earth, nominally four weeks after launch, bringing back not only the two-man crew but cassettes of film and experimental equipment.

MOL itself would never return, any additional use requiring a completely new laboratory, but it was perceived as the beginning to an expanding series of increasingly more advanced orbiting facilities.

Plans included very large orbital bases, one Top Secret planning document outlining a twelve-man space-based command post with a mass of 165,000lb (74,844kg) for 1975, and a still larger facility for 40 crew members weighing 470,000lb (213,192kg) for 1980.

MOL flights were open-ended and involved a gradual build-up in capabilities, with the more advanced stations consisting of several separate modules docked together. NASA had wanted Gemini as a precursor for developing rendezvous and docking, spacewalking and long duration flights before they were able to use Apollo. The Air Force wanted to use Gemini capsules to familiarise their pilots with space flight and to gain experience before they began flying MOL missions. To do that, in 1962 the Air Force anticipated a series of seven flights with Blue Gemini spacecraft.

A Titan IIIC lifts the Gemini GT-2 re-entry module with a heat-shield hatch on a test flight to qualify the concept on 19 January 1965.

The first two Blue Gemini missions would fly much the same missions as NASA Gemini flights, but with a US Air Force co-pilot. Two more flights would follow with an all-Air Force crew, preceding three flights for Air Force equipment involving an astronaut manoeuvring unit (AMU), a jet-pack that would allow a spacewalking astronaut to fly around outside the spacecraft. Other experiments pertinent to Air Force requirements could also be carried, such as an erectable ground-mapping radar.

NASA was the winner here, as the government formally approved NASA's own space station – Skylab – which would be launched in May 1973 after the last of six Moon landings, visited by three Apollo crews in that and the following year. As for NASA's Gemini, there were only ever ten manned flights flown in 1965 and 1966. Throughout this period and beyond, McDonnell presented a wide range of possible applications, and these demonstrated how versatile Gemini was.

Amid all the government programmes posited, cancelled or accepted, in 1963 the Douglas Aircraft Company proposed to NASA a Manned Orbital Research Laboratory (MORL) that would be serviced and supplied by modified Gemini spacecraft. The equipment section would be greatly expanded, provided with greatly enlarged cargo space, and capable of carrying up to six astronauts. Two would

be in a largely unchanged re-entry module similar to all Gemini missions, and a further four in a pressurised and enlarged equipment module behind. McDonnell also designed an unmanned cargo module with all crew provisions stripped out.

By 1967 NASA began developing leftover Apollo hardware for what would become the Skylab space station. But McDonnell had one other proposal: a version of the two-man Gemini spacecraft called Big-G that could carry up to twelve astronauts to a space station in Earth orbit. But the decision had already been made to abandon Gemini and use Apollo for any future supply missions, hence it was that spacecraft that rotated crew members to Skylab.

The twelve-man Big-G would have had a total launch weight of 37,700lb (17,100kg) with a length of 35.75ft (10.9m) and a maximum diameter of 21.66ft (6.6m) at the base of the greatly expanded Equipment Module. As proposed in 1967, McDonnell Douglas, as it was rebadged following a merger in April that year, forecast availability for manned flights in April 1971, supporting what NASA called its Apollo Applications Program (AAP), which had already resulted in the development of Skylab. But prudently merging Big-G with the AAP schedule, it suggested this spacecraft for ferry duties to the second workshop, which at this time NASA planned to launch after Skylab.

The Gemini B spacecraft would have been used for the US Air Force MOL programme, which was cancelled before flight operations could start.

MODELLING AN AIR FORCE GEMINI

With the success of the Gemini spacecraft that could carry two crew, ideas of follow-on missions that could involve larger craft were not far behind. One major project would have been the MOL, which used a Gemini as its 'ferry craft'. Some plans involved a larger version of Gemini itself, dubbed Big Gemini, while others were the standard Gemini, and some were even adapted to carry more than two crew.

These plans varied widely, but one intriguing design fell under the military banner, and consequently the United States Air Force. (A 'US Space Force' had yet to be thought about.) This design used a Gemini whose retro-rocket and equipment modules were converted to have fold-out doors where experiments, sensors and even weapons could be deployed.

This was attached to the final stage of a launch rocket, most likely a Gemini-Titan II, with some more equipment contained in the uppermost part of the stage, the rest being fuel for the two rocket motors.

The Build

For this build you need basically two sections: a Gemini kit and tubing, and motors to build the rocket stage. Of the two Gemini spacecraft generally available – Revell's in 1:48 and 1:24 scales – this conversion would be feasible with either. However, the larger scale, the 1:24 scale kit, is more spectacular, and was chosen here.

The three elements of the Gemini spacecraft are all used, though the aft two are modified considerably. By one of those convenient coincidences, in 1:24 scale the diameter of the aft end of the Equipment Module (EM) is almost exactly 5in – slightly less convenient in metric, as it is about 127mm – which makes the rocket stage diameter also 5in. Consequently, a piece of tubing with a diameter of 5in needs to be located.

The main materials used for this build are a Revell 1:24-scale Gemini spacecraft, and a length of EMA tube, 5in (127mm) in diameter.

After carefully measuring and marking out, the EMA tube (or any tube) can be cut with the razor saw. The idea is not to cut through in one go – rather, aim to build up the cut as you go round, following the marker line. This means that if you are ever slightly off the line, you will be able to regain it. Then, assuming your measuring and marking were accurate, and you follow the line exactly with the saw, you should end up with a clean cut!

The easiest – though most expensive – source is EMA tubing, where 5in diameter is a standard size (code VT500), but it is not cheap, and the availability of EMA products does vary from time to time. Other cheaper sources are standard household piping, used for rainwater downpipes and the like. Unfortunately 5in is not a standard size generally available, and most are a lot smaller.

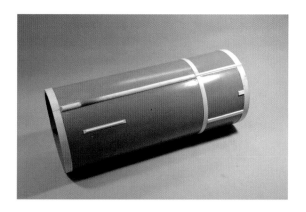

Detailing the exterior of the rocket stage, using strip plastic.

Cutting a square of sheet plastic to block the opening for the original command module engine bell.

Sorting out potential parts for the 'engine' end of the rocket stage. Here are the upper and lower bulkheads from the Monogram 1:32-scale Apollo CSM. In the end the engine bulkhead (lower) was used, and two Space Shuttle Main Engine (SSME) nozzles from a 1:72-scale Shuttle Orbiter.

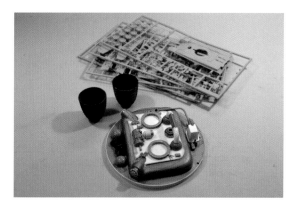

Fitting various parts – usually called 'widgets' – in place around the engine end of the rocket stage. In the background are various runners from 1:72-scale military kits, tanks and the like, which provide the widgets, and are invaluable for this type of detailing.

One option could be cardboard tube, though again, 5in is a larger size than would usually be available for such as sending rolled-up posters through the mail. Another option could be to 'roll your own', using plastic sheet, rolled round 5in circles of wood – or in fact slightly smaller, as the thickness of the plastic sheet has to be taken into account. The exact length of this upper rocket stage is not really important, so the 5in-diameter EMA tubing was cut to 12in (305mm) long – but slightly shorter or slightly longer is not going to make a great deal of difference to the final model.

The outer surface of the rocket stage is kept fairly simple. Some thin strips of thin plastic sheet were cut to wrap round the stage, both circular and lengthways. Again the exact pattern does not really matter. Some patterned plastic sheet could also be used as complete wraps (similar to those found on, for example, the stages of the Saturn V) – or just use strips of plain plastic. Some half-round tubing can also be used as conduits.

EMA actually does make 'half round' tube parts, but complete tube can be very carefully cut lengthways to create half-round tube. This is tricky and really needs a bandsaw, but short lengths could be done with a handsaw. More detailing for the exterior surface can be done later with paint and decals.

Building the Two Ends

What is going to be required in more detail are the two ends. The 'business' end – that is, the rocket motors – can use to advantage the fact that the internal diameter of the EMA 5in-diameter tube is 4¾in (120mm; the wall thickness of these largest EMA tubes is ⅛in [3mm]). By coincidence this is virtually the diameter of the Monogram 1:32-scale Apollo Command Service Module. Here, the top of the bottom bulkheads of the cylindrical Service

Module could be used as a base for the engine plate for this model.

The actual base plate of the Monogram kit is probably the best as a starting point. It really needs its diameter enlarging slightly, but frankly a strip of 1mm-thick plastic sheet is adequate. The inside of whatever tubing you have used (EMA or otherwise) needs to be fitted with stops to hold this disc in place and prevent it falling straight down the tube! A strip of plastic could be used, or several blocks of plastic (three is the minimum), glued just inside the tube, on which the engine plate will sit.

The Engine Bells

The Monogram 1:32 engine bell itself is far too large to be used, so the engine bells used here came from the Revell 1:72-scale Shuttle Orbiter, though the Monogram 1:72-scale Orbiter versions are equally suitable. The hole (for its own rocket bell) of the Command Service Module (CSM) base plate was covered with some thick (2mm) plastic sheet, and two EMA 1in-diameter rings (VX-32) were glued in place to take the Orbiter engines.

The surround area was then detailed using the usual approach of widgets out of the bits and pieces box. One very useful source of such widgets is military tank kits, both 1:35 and – used here – 1:72/1:76. All

A Gemini Equipment Module is test-fitted into the top of the rocket body. A built module is on the left.

The Gemini module is cut along the line where it matched the internal diameter of the tube, and the excess cut away.

the runners of these kits have a myriad of 'bits' that can be glued in place so they 'look light', and when sprayed one overall colour (here, Humbrol Metallic Gun Metal) 'everything is pulled together' and you then forget what the original parts were and where they were from. A misted top coat of aluminium was then sprayed on. The engine bells were first sprayed matt black, then bronze, then finally glued into place.

Fitting Out the Equipment Bay

The other end of the rocket stage has an equipment bay fitted inside that fills the interior and stretches down inside the rocket stage to a certain distance. This exact length doesn't really matter – one assumes most of the space in the rocket stage would be fuel tanks. A straightforward option to fill this space is to use the EM from another Gemini kit. Here it was turned the other way round and temporarily fitted into the tube. The excess round the original aft edge, now the forward edge, is trimmed to the diameter of the tubing. It can be accurately measured with a rule, but levelling up by eye will likely be adequate. Then cut round with a razor saw. This will remove about ¾in (20mm).

Most of the original equipment for the Gemini can then be fitted inside into the original locations on the 'floor'. Here the fuel tanks were doubled up from yet another Gemini kit, along with other tanks and equipment, to fill the remaining gaps. One extra piece of equipment shown in the diagram is a mass sensor probe that extends out through the open hatch, forward of the spacecraft itself. A support for this can be cemented to the floor of the 'reversed' EM, as close to the wall as is feasible – otherwise it won't extend through the new hatch. Then the long tube, made from EMA/Plastruct – though it could be metal tube, aluminium or brass – can pass through the opening. This is fitted after all the main assembly has taken place.

Building the Gemini Spacecraft

The Gemini spacecraft itself can be built as standard – there is no indication that it would be different to those that actually flew. The interiors of all flight Gemini were a light mid-grey, so there is no reason to think that this one would be any different.

The exterior of the Gemini spacecraft itself is of course black (not the oft-quoted 'dark blue': *see* also Chapter 1 on the Mercury Observatory). Here,

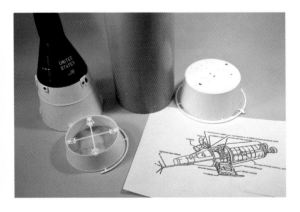

Examining some of the main elements against one of the very few artist impressions of this proposal. The built Revell Gemini, upper left, is used for reference throughout the construction, but another one was used for the actual build.

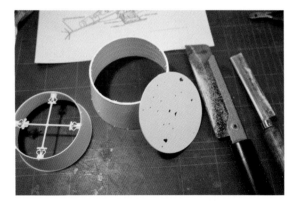

Removing the bulkhead of the equipment module of the Gemini. The saw cut was made along the indented lip of this section, which resulted in a clean removal of this 'disc'. It isn't needed for this build, so consign it to the bits and pieces box!

The two original Gemini modules – the retro rocket section and the equipment section (now without its end bulkhead) – are cemented together and, once thoroughly dry, the area for the two opening hatches is marked out. Their precise size does not matter too much, but they do take a fair percentage of the surface of these now joined modules.

Using the modelling razor saw, the hatches are carefully cut out from the joined modules.

Humbrol Satin Black was applied over a matt black primer coat, with a mist coat of metallic black (#201) over the top. There is an option of masking the tip of the forward section and spraying this silver. The interior can then be fitted, ensuring the hatches are in place as they are held by the interior, and the heat shield glued in place. The rim of this is painted matt red, and although the heat shield itself would be a metallic bronze, as it isn't really seen, the whole lot was sprayed matt red.

The majority of the work has to be done on the other two sections on a conventional Gemini – the

Just some of the 'bits and pieces' you get with the Revell 1:24-scale Gemini kit, with some duplicates here. These will be used to populate the new versions of the modules.

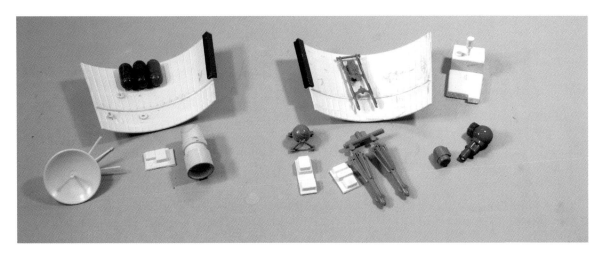

Choosing some equipment to fit the opening hatch door of the modified equipment module. These include the S-Band antenna from the Airfix 1:72 Lunar Module kit (far left).

retro-rocket section and the Equipment Module. The first task is to remove the base of the Equipment Module. The easiest method is carefully to saw the base off 'sideways', using the lip as a guide. The alternative would be to cut through vertically, but this would require even more care, and the inner edge would likely need far more cleaning up.

The two modules then need cementing together, and the join needs to be strong and secure. This is because when this is thoroughly dry the two opening 'hatches' need to be marked and cut out, and this opening goes across both modules. The precise dimensions of these hatches are not given, but they take up a fair percentage of the external surface. Here the length was 2¼in (57mm) and the width – across the diameter – 3¼in (83mm). The hatches then need very carefully sawing out, using a razor saw. There could be the option of hinging these panels/doors, but there's really not that much point, as all detail will be hidden. Consequently, lengths of L-shaped girder were cemented along the 'lower' (this is relative, as there is no 'up or down' in space!) edges, though they won't be attached to the main body until nearer the end of the construction.

The exterior of these two, now one, modules was fitted with the supplied exterior thrusters and attachment points. The latter are mainly to support the body of the main Gemini craft, which has tags on the heat shield that match with slots in the thruster bodies. This means the Gemini itself can be placed on the end of what was the retro-rocket module, and with a slight twist, the tags fit the slots and hold the Gemini in place.

Fitting Out the Two New Hatches

Regarding the two new 'hatches', exactly what to fit on these two hatch doors is really down to the modeller. The scant details that do exist indicate a range of various monitoring sensors: 'photographic camera', 'negation missiles', 'nuclear sensor' and 'radar', though the exact details are not really important. However, the 'radar' is a dish, and was replicated with the S-Band antenna found in the Airfix Lunar Module kit. Its stance was modified so it faced directly outwards (the kit stance is angled upwards), and locating circles for the three legs, cut from tube and glued to the inside of the starboard door. It appears this craft carried anti-satellite missiles (the 'negation missiles'), so two were found in a Hasegawa aircraft accessory pack, along with suitable launch rails.

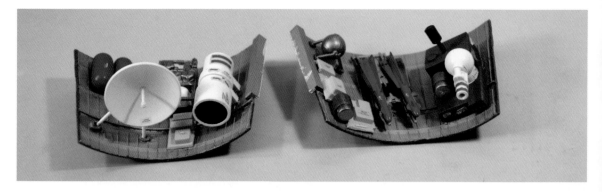

The opening hatch doors with the painted and decaled equipment in place. The exact layout of what is there isn't detailed, but there would have been the radar dish, telescope, maybe even anti-satellite missiles, the latter fitted to the right hatch, in red.

Some of the spare Gemini Equipment Module items were also relocated to these inner doors, and others made up from parts supplied in the MPC Pilgrim Observer space station kit. The telescope and camera items from that kit were particularly useful. Small decals can also be scattered around these pieces of equipment. Most aircraft decal sheets have suitable small decals intended for panels and the like, which you can't actually read, but nevertheless are there to 'look right'.

Painting the Modules

The Gemini spacecraft has these two aft sections in white, but as this is a military craft, something more, well 'military', was decided upon. The exterior ended up being sprayed Testor intermediate blue, which is more 'grey' than 'blue' and certainly less bright than 'white', and would seem more suitable for a military craft. The exterior was then masked and the interior,

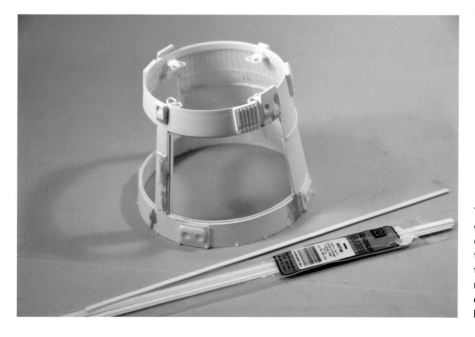

Thin plastic strips can be fitted to the edge of the openings for the hatches of this new equipment module. These inside edges will eventually be hand-painted red.

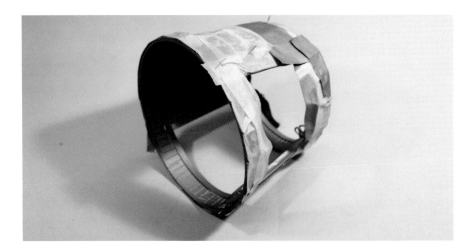

The exterior of the equipment module has been painted intermediate blue, and now masked so the inner surface can be sprayed aluminium.

Decals for the rocket stage, here from Monogram's 1:48-scale Hustler. Other aircraft decal sheets supplied smaller markings.

including the inner surfaces of the hatches, sprayed aluminium.

Intermediate blue was also used as the base coat for the rocket stage. When dry, areas were then masked off to create individual panels, and the whole stage was then over-sprayed aluminium.

The masking was then removed to reveal the 'intermediate blue' panels. The interior edge of the actual Gemini hatches is matt red, and this was followed through to the new hatches, which were also given red edges.

With the new 'equipment' section of Gemini completed and the hatch doors glued in place, this whole section can then be cemented on to the end of the rocket section. This is best done by standing the rocket stage on end, placing the equipment section in place, lining it up so the position of the telescopic mass sensor will pass through the port hatch, and applying cement through these doors to the join around the top of the rocket stage. Then allow the cement to dry thoroughly, because when displayed it is likely to be horizontal (so at right angles to the upright), and with the main Gemini in place, there will be quite a lot of strain on this join.

Applying Decals

Either before or after this, decals can be applied to the exterior. The ones here, the large 'USAF',

'United States Air Force' and US Stars and Bars national markings, came from Monogram's 1:48-scale Hustler decal sheets. The Hustler in 1:48 scale is a large model, so the decals are equally impressive. However, there are many aftermarket decal sheets that will have suitable markings. The Gemini craft itself can retain its UNITED STATES decals, with maybe the Stars and Stripes as well.

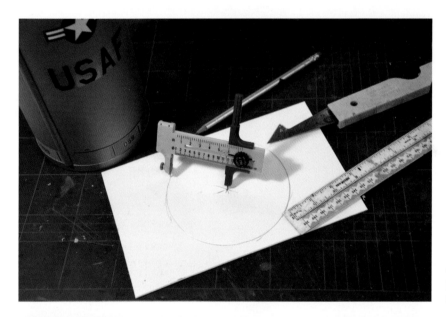

Cutting the circles out of plastic sheet to make a support stand.

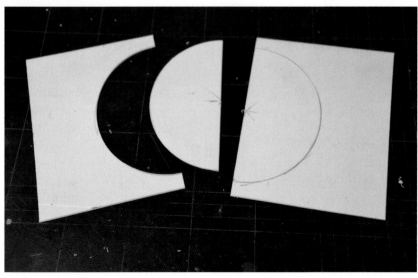

The resulting semicircles, snapped away to leave cradle-shaped sections, that will form the stand.

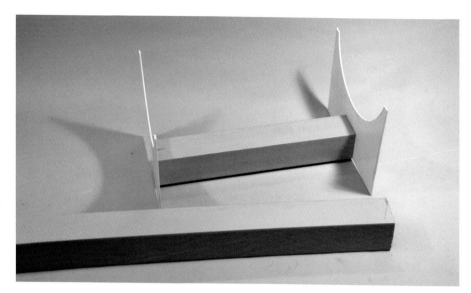

These cradles were attached to a piece of square tubing, which was itself cemented to an MDF wood base and painted Humbrol midnight blue.

Displaying the Model

The finished model is quite large and heavy, so will need some method of support for display. One way is to cut two semi-circles out of plastic sheet, of the diameter of the rocket stage (in this case,

5in [127mm]). Trim these down to a suitable size and attach them to a central bar (here a length of square EMA moulding), and fix that on to a base, here MDF board. Then prime and paint a suitable 'support base' colour – in this example, Humbrol Midnight Blue.

The finished 'Military Gemini' on its base. Note the extended mass sensor probe that protrudes forwards out through the port hatch towards the end of the Gemini nose. The interior of the forward end of the rocket stage, where the extra equipment from another Gemini kit has been fitted, can be viewed through the open hatches.

The finished 'Military Gemini' on its base. Note the small areas of Intermediate Blue colouring on the main rocket body and the bronze rocket bells.

The finished 'Military Gemini'. Another view of the extended mass sensor probe, and the various pieces of equipment fitted to the new hatches.

CHAPTER 5

X-15 PIGGYBACK ON A VALKYRIE

Beginning in the mid-1950s, the Air Force, the Navy and NASA's predecessor, the National Advisory Committee for Aeronautics (NACA), decided to build a hypersonic research aircraft. Beginning with Chuck Yeager's shattering of the sound barrier in October 1947, several experimental rocket-powered research aircraft had demonstrated speeds up to Mach 3. Now was the time to push on to at least Mach 7, which called for a very special type of aircraft. Designated X-15, it was launched from beneath the wing of an eight-jet, Boeing B-52 bomber.

Initial flights were made with an interim propulsion system involving two rocket motors, each with four combustion chambers, designated the XLR-11. Later flights would be powered by the XLR-99, producing a thrust of around 57,000lb (235.5kN) and capable of pushing the X-15 beyond Mach 6. In all, the X-15 conducted 199 flights by the end of the programme in October 1968. Only one aircraft was destroyed (X-15-3) and its pilot killed in an unfortunate accident on 15 November 1967 when it went out of control and crashed.

The X-15 dropping away from the underside of the wing of the B-52 carrier plane, one of 199 flights conducted from Edwards Air Force Base, California.

The second X-15 was rebuilt and equipped with external propellant tanks for a longer burn time from its rocket motor. Later, a white-coated thermal insulation was applied for high-speed flights beyond Mach 6.

On 9 November 1962 an accident caused X-15-2 to flip over on landing, almost crushing the pilot as his head contacted the ground. Originally, the X-15 had been designed to reach Mach 7, although it never exceeded Mach 5 in its original configuration. In rebuilding the No. 2 aircraft for planned flights to the elusive Mach 7 it was extended in length and fitted with two external propellant tanks. The tanks would be used first before the fuel from the interior of the X-15 after which the external tanks were jettisoned. Designated X-15A-2 it made several high-speed flights, reaching a maximum of Mach 6.7 on 3 October 1967; but it experienced significant damage due to parts of the structure melting from heat generated by friction with the atmosphere.

High-altitude flights took the X-15 to the very edge of space, the maximum altitude achieved being 354,000ft (107,900m) on 22 August 1963. This was approximately ten times the height achieved by a commercial airliner on an intercontinental flight, and it registered the pilot, Joe Walker, as an astronaut. It is an internationally recognised world record for a winged aircraft, and one that has never been

exceeded. Also with wings, the Space Shuttle of 1981–2011 was a spacecraft powered into orbit by solid propellant rockets: it is not considered a powered aircraft. But even this was not enough for a lot of the information both NASA and the Air Force sought. For more ambitious goals, an X-15B was proposed.

The X-15B would have been launched from the ground by clusters of solid propellant rockets, and would have conducted a single orbit of the Earth before returning. But it was limited in that it would have been required to ditch in the Gulf of Mexico, the pilot having to eject to safety on the way down. The idea of the X-15B never really went away, and early in the 1960s other methods of launch were considered, including replacing the B-52 carrier plane with the XB-70 Valkyrie.

While the X-15 was a highly advanced research programme, it emerged in parallel with studies by the US Air Force into a high-flying, super-fast strategic bomber capable of long-distance cruising at three times the speed of sound. Named XB-70 Valkyrie, it had a sustained speed of Mach 3 at high altitude, and was to be powered by six General

The XB-70 Valkyrie was designed as a bomber for delivering nuclear warheads and also for reconnaissance, but consideration was given to it carrying a delta-wing X-15.

Electric YJ93-GE-3 turbojet engines, each delivering a thrust of 28,000lb (124.5kN) or 19,000lb (84.5kN) with afterburner. At take-off, the XB-70 would put out a total thrust of 114,000lb (507kN), and achieve Mach 3 cruise by riding on its own shock wave, a concept known as 'compression lift'.

Rolled out in May 1964, the XB-70 was unlike anything that had appeared in public before. It had a length of 189ft (57.6m), a wingspan of 105ft (32m), and a total height to the tip of its twin vertical fins of 30ft (9.1m). With its delta platform swept back 65 degrees, the wing had an area of 6,297sq ft (585sq m), about the size of two tennis courts. The outer wing sections were hinged so they could be deflected down at an angle of up to 70 degrees,

improving directional stability and rebalancing the centre of pressure at Mach 3. The first flight took place on 21 September and was followed by the second aircraft on 17 July 1965.

Redundant to purpose, the XB-70 programme was cancelled, but the two prototypes were kept flying for their value as research aircraft into sustained Mach 3 flight. This is where a delta-wing X-15 came in. While the B-52 was still considered the optimum carrier for delta-wing developments, the advantage of launching off the back of the XB-70 travelling at Mach 3 was self-evident! Moreover, the X-15 derivative could lift off the XB-70 at altitudes approaching 80,000ft (24,400m), almost twice the height when launched off a B-52.

MODELLING THE DELTA-WINGED X-15 AND THE XB-70

It is a reasonably straightforward task to build a model of one of the most exotic aircraft combos ever devised, if not actually flown: that of the delta-winged version of the X-15, with the XB-70

Valkyrie. This is because both craft have existed as commercial model kits, in the same scale of 1:72.

The arrival of the 1:72-scale kit of the XB-70 in 1995 was a surprise, as not only is it very large in this scale, but it came from what was ostensibly a model car company, that of AMT. Actually AMT had produced aircraft kits before, 1930s-type civilian plans such as the Stinson Reliant and Lockheed Vega, and

Three boxes of the Monogram 1:72-scale X-15. The bottom box is the Revell reissue of the Monogram kit, *not* its own original kit.

70

The box for the newer 1:72-scale X-15 from MPM (part of the Czech Special Hobby empire).

The box for one of the two AMT issues of the XB-70.

had issued the first ever model kit of USS *Enterprise* from *Star Trek*, and the five-part 'Man in Space' set in 1:200 scale with – at that time – all five crewed American space launchers. However, the move to aerospace military hardware was a slight surprise.

The overall length of the complete model is 31.5in (800mm), and consists of a modest (for these days) 75 parts. The kit is actually still available, though now under another model name – that of Italeri, acquired through various takeovers.

The delta-winged X-15

Given the prominence of probably the most famous 'X plane' of all time, it took a long time for the North American X-15 to be made as a conventional 1:72-scale kit. This was possibly because one of the very earliest Revell kits was an X-15. But it wasn't 1:72, it was 1:65. This is reasonably close, but for the purist, not close enough. This came about because in the early days of Revell – and admittedly a number of other American model kit companies – kits were not always built to a generally accepted

The start of the modifications of the Monogram X-15 – removing the wings using a razor saw, two sizes of which are shown.

Marking out the shape of the now wingless X-15 fuselage on stock styrene sheet...

...then drawing out a suitable delta shape – the exact shape is not really important as there were so many of them, and none were built anyway!

scale, but instead were built to 'fit the box'. It actually took Airfix to set the standard, as (virtually) all its kits have always been 'constant scale'. Up until then, for the Americans model kit boxes were only made to certain sizes for cost savings, so the companies chose the nearest size box and then made the kit to fit.

So for many years this was the closest a modeller could get to an accurate 1:72-scale X-15. There was a vacuum-formed kit from Airmodell, but vac-formed kits invariably need specialist modelling skills to build. Consequently it took until 1987 for a correct 1:72-scale X-15 kit to be released by Monogram, and then several more decades before another came along, from the Czech company MPM.

Two specialist manufacturer models of an 'updated X-15' have been made in 1:72 scale, one from Fantastic Plastic, for the proposed 'X-15D', though the shape is very different to the X-15 itself,

while Sharkit in France made an X-15 'DeltaWing Proposal', which shows the upturned wingtips. However, this is a desktop-type model with no cockpit details or undercarriage – not that the latter would be necessary for the craft attached to the top of the XB-70.

Consequently it is easiest to use the Monogram or MPM kit. Most recently the Monogram was released under the Revell name, so ensure that any 'Revell'-labelled kit is in the new artwork box and has '1:72' as the scale – otherwise it is the older 1:65-scale kit.

Both the Monogram and MPM kits represent the lengthened X-15-A2 version that had 29in (740mm) added to the fuselage length. Most delta-wing proposals are based on this X-15-A2, so using the lengthened version is a good starting point. In fact some proposals called for an even longer fuselage, an increase of 10ft (3m), in which case you will need two kits, cutting each in half lengthways, but adding a scale '10ft', which for either kit (which is already a scale 29in [740mm] longer) requires an additional 1.25in (30mm) of fuselage length. So adjust the two sections accordingly.

All these 'future' plans show a delta wing, but the details can vary, especially with the wingtips. Some plans have the wingtips with an upward sweep, some are swept down, and others have a cruciform shape. Some have wingtips in pairs above and below the wings, and yet others were purely plain

deltas. But frankly, as the X-15 delta-wing variants were never built, and any drawings and plans vary considerably, you can more or less choose you own pattern.

The Plain Delta Conversion

The 'plain delta' is the easiest conversion. This just requires some styrene sheet stock, available from model or hobby shops, and also obtainable online,

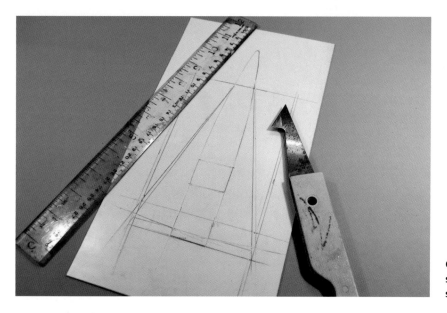

Cutting out the styrene sheet, using a suitable scoring knife.

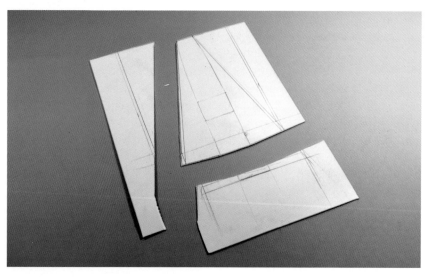

Removing the excess styrene.

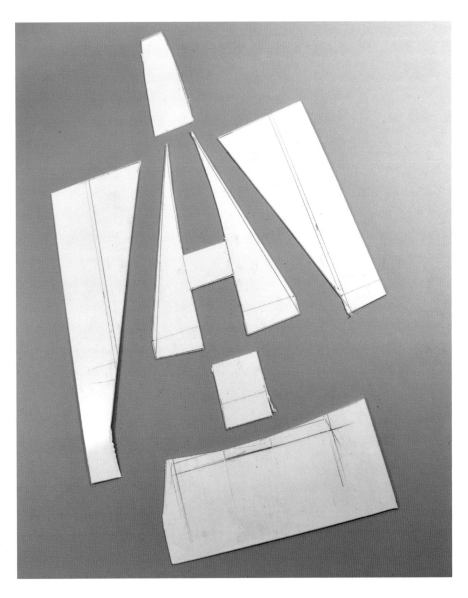

**The final shape –
centre – surrounded by
the removed styrene
sheet.**

as such shops tend to be few and far between these days in all countries.

The X-15 can be assembled according to the instructions, except the lower fin and tailplanes are not fitted. The existing wings also need removing. These are attached to the upper half of the split fuselage. (Unlike the majority of aircraft kits, the split is horizontal, not vertical.)

The next task is to cut the new wings from styrene sheet of about 1.5 to 2mm thickness. Because the

fuselage line is not straight, lay either half on the styrene and pencil round the outline. It will certainly be stronger if both wings are cut from the same sheet, and left joined with a strip of styrene in the middle. When this is cut out, lay it over the X-15 fuselage halves and mark where the plastic of these halves needs to be filed with a 'slot' to take this supporting strip.

As none of these versions was ever built, the exact angle of the new delta wings does not matter too

The wings are connected by the central strip for strength. This is marked on the X-15 fuselage, using a chrome pen here as it shows up on the black plastic of the X-15. The 'slot' can then be filed out to take this strip.

Embossed plastic sheet was used to create the 'corrugated' finish suggested for some proposals.

much; however, generally they stretch back from the cockpit bulge almost to the aft of the plane. The leading edges of the wings need thinning to a sharp edge; the trailing edges also need thinning, but to a lesser degree. Elevons then need scribing into the trailing edge.

Adding Wingtips

At this point you need to decide if the craft remains in this configuration, or whether you are going to add wingtips. Two versions were built for this conversion: one is purely the delta shape with no fins, while the

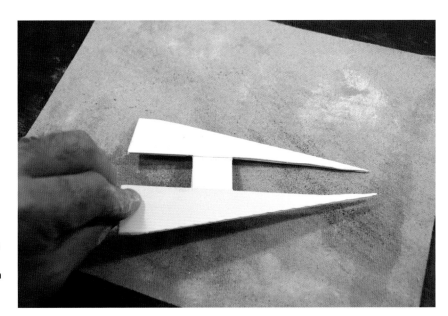

Sanding the leading edges of the delta sheet, using sanding paper glued down to a plywood backing board.

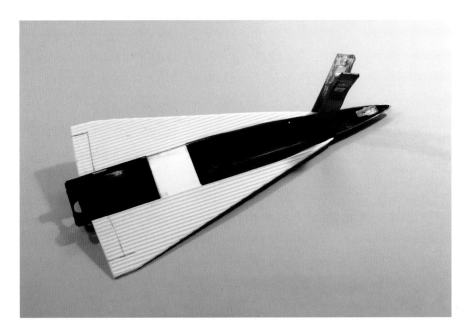

Attaching the new wings to the lower fuselage – a clamp is used here in one area of the leading edge.

other includes fins. These were proposed for some versions to replace the effect of the loss of the lower section of the main fin. The simplest wingtips are the ones that are fixed to the upper surface only, and angle out from the vertical at around 10 degrees. Other plans show winglets top and bottom, but set in by a few inches from the actual wingtip.

Some drawings of this version also show the upper wing surfaces covered in a corrugated pattern, which is the second version built here. The corrugation comes from patterned styrene sheet: this is first glued to the upper delta shape (it isn't clear if it would be on the underside as well) and once dry, it is carefully cut round, and the edges thinned to match

Cutting the new upper and lower outer fins. These are cut from the ailerons on the original wings that have been removed.

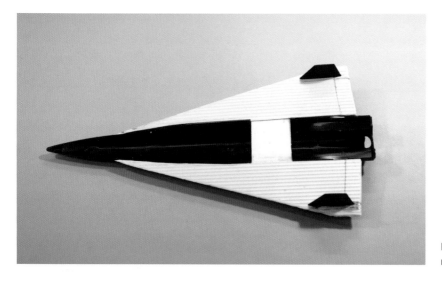

Fitting the outer fins to the new wings.

the main wing, using a sharp knife, small files and a final sanding.

The top and bottom fuselage halves are then fitted in place, not forgetting the cockpit interior, fitted to the top half. However, there is frankly no point in adding any detail to this, or the seat, as no details can be seen with the canopy in place, as the only clear section is the tiny teardrop-shaped window.

The join between the new wings and the fuselage will likely need some model filler, which must be allowed to dry thoroughly before being wet-and-dry sanded to get a smooth, integrated finish.

The small fins for the outer wings were cut from the original tailplanes, as they are not being used, and these have the necessary thinning already built into the leading edges. So the two shapes can be cut from each original tailplane, and then glued into place on the top and bottom of the wing. Again the precise shape is not really important as they only existed in drawings.

The remainder of the X-15 can then be completed according to the instructions, omitting the lower fin. However, the engine nozzle would certainly be different, being much larger than the existing X-15s. Here, an engine bell from a 1:144-scale Airfix Apollo Service Module was used – though the SSME Orbiter engine bells in any 1:144-scale space shuttle kit could also be suitable.

Pretty in Pink

The finish for this 'Delta X-15' is the same black as the existing X-15s, and the Inconel X surface can be matched by a satin black spray over a matt black base, then topped with a thin mist coat of metallic black. It is entirely possible that had these X-15 delta wings been built, they would have been covered in ablative material, many versions of which were experimented with on various flights. The most

famous – and most distinctive – was the all-white as depicted in the Monogram kit, which itself was white over a pink ablative material. But all the drawings and images of potential Delta X-15s show the standard black finish that was used here.

The markings would also certainly generally match those on the existing X-15s, so those in the kit can be used.

THE XB-70

The AMT (now Italeri) XB-70 can basically be built 'out of the box', though you have to decide if the undercarriage is to be built retracted or lowered, and if the outer wing sections are to be positioned horizontally, or 'lowered'. As with many of these aircraft kits – particularly the large ones – there is no stand provided, ruling out a flying stance, unless

Building the XB-70 can involve some filler on the wing roots – not uncommon with an aircraft kit of this size.

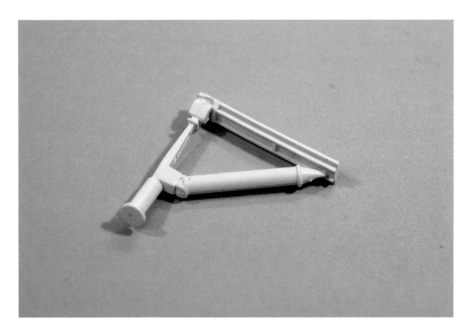

Scratch-building the rear supports for the XB-70. These are built up from Shuttle Orbiter attachment parts from an Airfix Shuttle kit.

Two versions of the proposed delta-wing X-15, both built from Monogram X-15A-2 kits.

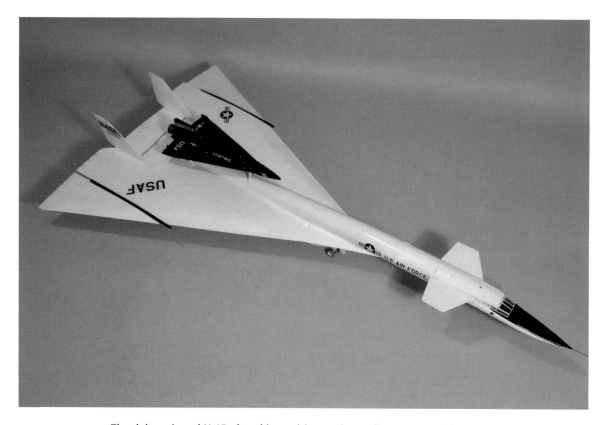

The delta-winged X-15 placed in position on its cradles on top of the XB-70.

a scratch-built stand is devised. Consequently it is easiest to build the aircraft before take-off, with the undercarriage lowered and the wings straight out. They would be anyway if the plane is on the ground, as the tips, when drooped, sit lower than the extended undercarriage!

Both the XB-70s that were built were white overall, with only the area in front of the cockpit being black. If the aircraft had gone into production, they would almost certainly have been in bare metal, therefore silver/aluminium in appearance, which is an option. However, the 'prototype' white finish was used here.

Because of the size of the parts, some filler was necessary along the areas where the wings meet the fuselage, though this is quite common with many model plane kits of this size. The markings include

NASA and the registration of the remaining XB-70 that is (genuinely!) '20001'. This plane now resides in the Research and Experimental Aircraft Hanger at the USAF Museum in Dayton, Ohio.

The only actual modification required is of course the attachment for the X-15-3 to the top of the fuselage. Here, modified Airfix Space Shuttle kit parts were used, for the rear pair. These were built up using the parts where the Orbiter attaches to the External Tank. The forward support was modified from a wheel undercarriage strut from a 1:72 Revell Space Shuttle Orbiter.

The finished result is certainly spectacular, especially with the still futuristic look of the XB-70. Even 50 years on, it still looks amazing and would not be out of place in any science fiction movie.

CHAPTER 6

HOW THE SATURN IB GREW BIGGER

The Saturn family of space launch vehicles proposed in the 1950s was known as Juno V. Juno I had been the adapted Redstone rocket used for launching satellites, Juno II was the space launcher version of the Jupiter-A ballistic missile, and Jupiter III and IV were progressively more powerful developments of Juno II that never materialised. Juno V came in several categories designated A, B and C. Only the C-series proposed the use of highly efficient cryogenic upper stages, and the C-1 (later known as Saturn I) was

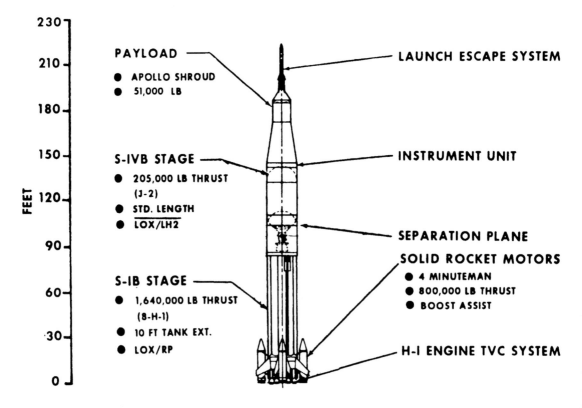

A 25 per cent increase in lift capacity for the Saturn IB would have been achieved by a lengthened first stage to extend its burn time, adding four Minuteman booster rockets to increase thrust.

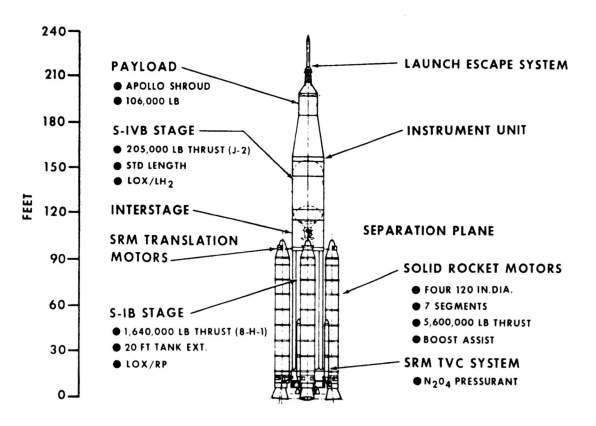

PAYLOAD
- APOLLO SHROUD
- 106,000 LB

S-IVB STAGE
- 205,000 LB THRUST (J-2)
- STD LENGTH
- LOX/LH$_2$

INTERSTAGE

SRM TRANSLATION MOTORS

S-IB STAGE
- 1,640,000 LB THRUST (8-H-1)
- 20 FT TANK EXT.
- LOX/RP

LAUNCH ESCAPE SYSTEM

INSTRUMENT UNIT

SEPARATION PLANE

SOLID ROCKET MOTORS
- FOUR 120 IN.DIA.
- 7 SEGMENTS
- 5,600,000 LB THRUST
- BOOST ASSIST

SRM TVC SYSTEM
- N$_2$O$_4$ PRESSURANT

FEET: 240 — 210 — 180 — 150 — 120 — 90 — 60 — 30 — 0

Extending the S-IB stage still further, uprating the H-1 engines and using four 120in (304.8cm) strap-on boosters raises the lift capacity by 120 per cent over a standard Saturn IB.

the first in a progressively more powerful range of rockets proposed as space launchers.

The C-1 and C-2 variants proposed a first-stage cluster of eight tanks built from the jigs for Juno I rockets surrounding a large central tank from jigs for the Juno II, powered by eight H-1 rocket motors with kerosene and liquid oxygen propellants. C-3 and C-4 variants used a completely new first stage powered by the F-1 rocket motor with two at the base of the C-3 and four at the base of the C-4. With a projected thrust of 1.5 million lb (6,672kN), the F-1 was almost eight times more powerful than the H-1, which had a thrust of 188,000lb (836.2kN). A further development of the C-4 would incorporate a fifth F-1 engine in the first stage, making it the C-5 – the famous Saturn V selected for Apollo Moon missions.

Saturn IB would have a greater payload capability due to its having a larger cryogenic second stage, the S-IVB, with a thrust of 200,000lb (889.6kN) from its one J-2 engine. The six RL-10 motors for the S-IV stage on Saturn I had a thrust of 90,000lb (400.3kN). The S-IVB stage was in development as the third stage for Saturn V and would have restart capabilities with the stage providing a much longer burn time.

Development of the Saturn IB into a more capable launch vehicle began in 1960 with a cryogenic Centaur stage to increase its ability to support deep-space missions. Centaur became the standard cryogenic upper stage for Atlas, Titan and subsequent derivatives down to the present, but it was never used with Saturn IB. NASA had a lot of prospective missions that would require an intermediate launch vehicle.

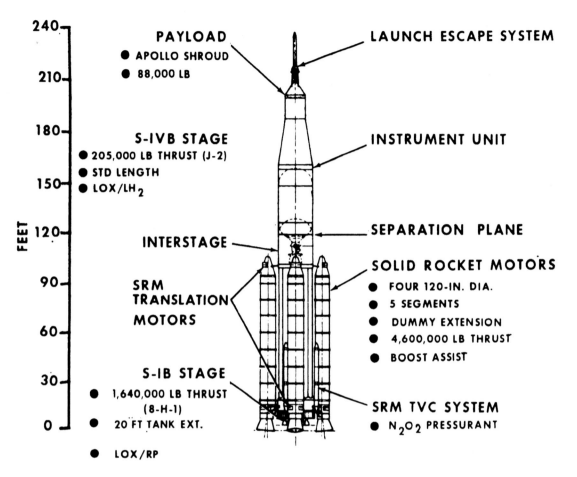

PAYLOAD
- APOLLO SHROUD
- 88,000 LB

LAUNCH ESCAPE SYSTEM

S-IVB STAGE
- 205,000 LB THRUST (J-2)
- STD LENGTH
- LOX/LH$_2$

INSTRUMENT UNIT

INTERSTAGE

SEPARATION PLANE

SRM TRANSLATION MOTORS

SOLID ROCKET MOTORS
- FOUR 120-IN. DIA.
- 5 SEGMENTS
- DUMMY EXTENSION
- 4,600,000 LB THRUST
- BOOST ASSIST

S-IB STAGE
- 1,640,000 LB THRUST (8-H-1)
- 20 FT TANK EXT.
- LOX/RP

SRM TVC SYSTEM
- N$_2$O$_2$ PRESSURANT

FEET — 240, 210, 180, 150, 120, 90, 60, 30, 0

With an extended S-IB stage, higher thrust H-1 engines and four 156in (396.2cm) solid propellant boosters, payload capacity grows by 165 per cent.

But the reality that the agency had little money beyond Apollo for doing all the things it wanted to had not yet dawned – and arguably never did.

By 1966 the potential payload manifest for the Saturn IB seemed large, and NASA reviewed possibilities for increasing payload capacity. With strap-on Solid Rocket Boosters attached, the Titan IIIC was available with a capacity for lifting 28,900lb (13,100kg) into Earth orbit – but this was slightly less than the existing Saturn IB at 37,000lb (16,783kg). There was great potential for developing Saturn IB into an intermediate launch vehicle capable of bridging the gap between Titan IIIC and the mighty

Saturn V, which had a payload capacity of 260,000lb (117,936kg). Nothing else existed to do that.

Different configurations were examined, and suitable options selected. Prime among these were the United Alliance (UL) 120in (304.8cm) Solid Rocket Boosters, each with a thrust of 1.15 million lb (5,115kN), the Minuteman ICBM first stage with a thrust of 200,000lb (889.6kN), and the 205,000lb (911.84kN) H-1 engines with ground- or air-start optional according to the overall thrust and loads.

The proposed MLV-11.5 would have had a lift-off thrust of 4.6 million lb (20,460kN), but the eight

H-1 engines would not have ignited until 1min 48sec into flight, 7sec before burnout and separation of the solids.

This configuration would have provided a payload capability of 74,000lb (33,566kg) to low Earth orbit, or 78,000lb (35,380kg) with a Centaur as third stage above the S-IVB. A variation on this would have used the same arrangement of solids, each with five segments, but with the S-IB first stage lengthened by 20ft (6.1m) to extend the burn duration of the eight H-1 engines. The added energy available would have increased payload capacity to 88,000lb (39,917kg).

The ultimate lift-capacity variant would have used the same extended-length S-IB stage but with four, seven-segment solid boosters delivering a launch thrust of 5.6 million lb (24,908kN) and delivering a payload of 106,000lb (48,082kg) to orbit.

Aerospace technology and management consultants Bellcom came up with a proposal that used the Rohr Corporation's 260in (6.6m) diameter solid propellant rocket, test-fired in 1965–67 but with no specific application. Developed jointly between NASA-Lewis and the Air Force, the 260in motor demonstrated a thrust of approximately 3.6 million lb (16,000kN). Designated Saturn IB-5A, the stage would have had a length of 137.4ft (41.8m) and required launch from a water-based table to dampen the enormous acoustic pressure waves from such a monster.

Plans to use the uprated variants of the Saturn IB were abandoned as irrelevant when on 1 August 1968 NASA cancelled long-lead procurement of items for future Saturn IBs. On 29 November 1968 NASA decided to close both launch pads (LC-34 and LC-37), the only ones built for this vehicle.

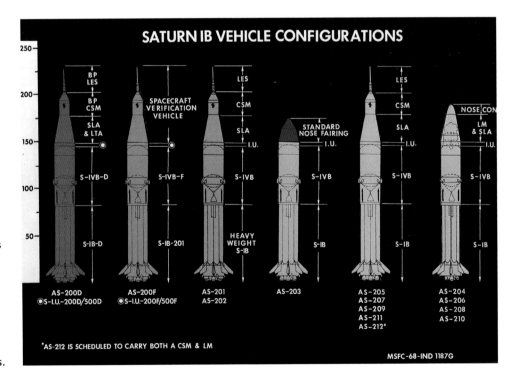

The various configurations of Saturn IB, including test flights, different payload fairings and spacecraft configurations.

MODELLING THE UPGRADED SATURN IB

With the majority of the Apollo project being centred round the giant Saturn V, it is easy to forget the smaller Saturn IB that launched the Apollo 7 crew. Plus, besides launching Apollo 7, there were four other launches with crews – the three crewed launches to Skylab, termed Skylab 2, 3 and 4, and the final launch as part of the Apollo Soyuz Test Project in 1975. Others that were launched without crews successfully carried such as the three Pegasus satellites, designed to study micrometeorite impacts on their giant extended panels that were 96ft (29m) long by 14ft (4.3m) wide, in preparation for the

The main boxes that you will see for the 1:144-scale Airfix Saturn IB – the first issue is on the left from 1979; at centre is the reissue from 1991; and on the right is the most recent, dating from 2011.

A built model that had seen better days was used for the 'boosters' conversion. Here the first stage was disassembled, the fin section removed (that needed slight persuasion), and all the engine bells removed from the engine bulkhead.

actual Apollo missions with the astronauts. But there were also other proposals.

As far as modellers are concerned, the slight problem is that there are very few models of the IB. The best known is the 1:144 scale from Airfix, and that has had varied distribution, but should be available, even if only from online auction sites. There is a Saturn IB in 1:200 from AMT, but it is only available as part of its 'Man in Space' set. (The Saturn V for the same set has been available as a separate kit, but not the IB.) There are also flying versions, the best

known from Estes, which make a very good static model, but will need extra work if you want to use such a kit for these conversions. Consequently any Saturn IB used here is almost certainly going to be down to the Airfix kit.

The Boosted Saturn IB

If the Saturn IB were to become the standard launcher for large uncrewed payloads for NASA, it would have needed additional boosters. There

The boosters came from the Heller Ariane 4 kit. The parts themselves sit on the box for the second issue under the Bobkit name. At the back are (left) the first issue, under the Bobcat name, and (right) under Heller's own name. The parts for the rocket itself are the same in all three kits, but whereas the Bobcat and Bobkit have a semblance of a launch pad included, the Heller issue is purely the rocket and a circular base.

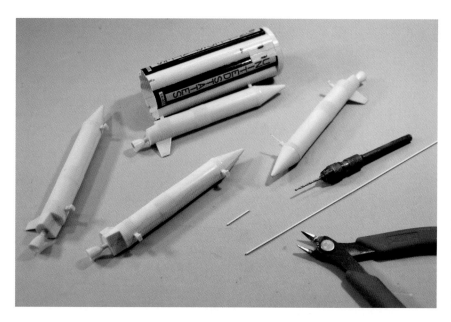

Assembling the parts for the boosters and the S-IB stage. The upper connection uses a length of thin rod, with holes drilled – using a pin vice – in the fuel-tank section.

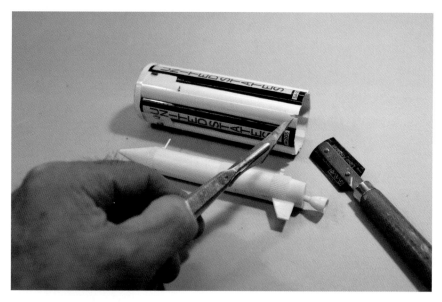

Close-up of cutting slots in the lower tank section of the Chrysler S-IB stage. The scalpel points to the slot that has been sawn out with the razor saw, right.

were plans for both solid and liquid boosters in several numbers, two, four and even eight, positioned around the Chrysler first stage of the launcher. One straightforward conversion is to add four booster rockets to the standard Saturn IB, and one source of such boosters is the Heller 1:125-scale Ariane 4 kit.

The Ariane 4 is a relatively simple kit, intended to be snapped together, though it can of course be glued. Each booster is purely two halves, so can be quickly assembled. Each has two attachment points, which can be adapted for their new use on the Saturn IB. First a slot needs to be cut at the base of every other tank of the main section, to take the lower attachment point

The boosters were painted white separately, as the S-IB stage, sprayed all white, covering the black panels. Decals were then added, the original vertical 'UNITED STATES' from the Saturn IB kit, and 'USA' from the S-IC stage of a Saturn V.

of the booster. If this is a new kit, this shouldn't be a problem. Just cement the two main halves together and mark the central point of every other tank.

If the conversion is being done with an already built kit that has seen better days (as it is in the photographs), ideally the lower section with the eight fins needs removing first. If this is too firmly glued in place and would be damaged if removal attempts were made, not all is lost. A slot can be created by drilling two small holes, one above the other, and filing out the gap in between. The top attachment point can be achieved in a similar way. Drill holes and file out, or purely trim the top attachment point, drill a hole, fit a short length of pipe or rod, and drill another matching hole in the tank.

With this first stage built, the upper stages could be anything you want. It could be the existing S-IVB stage with Apollo, and so capable of reaching

The complete booster-augmented Saturn IB, carrying the S-IVB stage and an Apollo craft. This set-up could have taken this particular Apollo into lunar orbit.

alternating black and white around the first-stage tanks, with UNITED STATES on a white background over the black areas, as available on the Airfix decal sheet. But in the last four crewed flights, Skylab 2, 3 and 4 and 'Apollo 18' (otherwise Apollo-Soyuz), the first stage was all white, with no black stripes down the main section. This saves masking and painting the black areas. Actually in all crewed cases, the interstage did have the alternative white and black, as did the fins. But overall – given that this version was never built – feel free to paint as you wish.

Saturn IB/Centaur

One future plan for the Saturn IB was to launch the Centaur upper stage. This would in effect become the main workhouse of NASA's planetary missions. But instead that task moved to the Titan family of launchers, and the Titan IIIE/Centaur was built and flew, launching such as the two Viking probes to Mars and the two Voyager probes to the outer planets. But the Saturn IB/Centaur could have been viable using the standard Chrysler S-IB first stage, the intersection, the S-IVB second stage, with the Centaur as the third stage.

This can be built using the payload shroud produced for the Airfix Skylab Saturn V kit. The diameter matches exactly – Skylab was, after all, a modified S-IVB stage anyway. In theory, all you would need to do is replace everything about the intersection of a Saturn IB with the Skylab section of that kit. However, that does have the modifications to the S-IVB stage done for Skylab, especially the folded solar arrays, so a neater option is to saw off the 'Skylab' S-IVB stage, and cement directly on the 'Saturn IB' S-IVB stage. The shape of the Skylab shroud is also quite a good match for what would be a Centaur shroud on a Saturn IB/Centaur set-up, even down to the nose section being a double cone. But even if it wasn't, we are back to the fact that this was an unbuilt design, so things could – and probably would – have changed.

lunar orbit, or it could be a completely new upper stage.

Incidentally, you can choose what colour scheme the Saturn IB is finished with. Most early flights, including Apollo 7, flew with the well-known

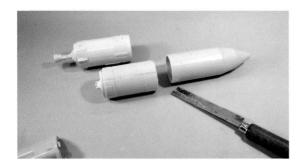

Removing the 'Skylab' for the upper stage of the Airfix Skylab Saturn V kit, to create a Centaur upper stage. In theory this could be left 'as is', as Skylab was an empty S-IVB stage anyway. But it has been remoulded to include Skylab details such as folded solar arrays, so instead it was replaced with an actual S-IVB stage (as included in both the Airfix Saturn V and IB kits), which of course is the same diameter and will attach directly to the Skylab fairing.

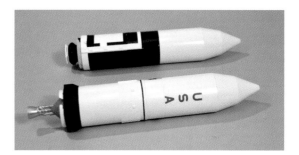

The new Centaur stage, compared to the Skylab (background). Even without the black paint, details do differ and the rocket engine of the S-IVB stage has been replaced with the radiator panel and tank section – though admittedly this would be hidden with this stage in position on the launcher.

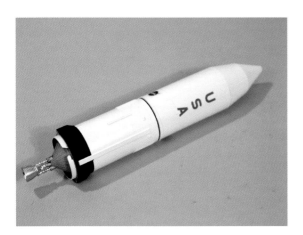

The painted and decaled Centaur upper stage for the Saturn IB. The lower black band usually featured on S-IVB stages has been retained, and new decals found for the Centaur section.

The paint scheme can either be the 'Apollo 7' scheme with the black and white tanks on the S-IB, or the 'all white' scheme. Decals can follow the ones supplied in the Airfix kit, and you have a choice if you want to add anything to the Centaur shroud.

The Centaur upper stage on the Saturn IB.

Saturn IB – X-15

Perhaps the most fanciful use of a Saturn IB launcher would be to launch the X-15! Although X-15s only flew using horizontal launch methods – that is, air-dropped from the B-52 mothership – the idea of a vertical launch was not an isolated idea. There was a proposal to use Navaho boosters as a vertical launch vehicle, or a cluster of three Titan I rockets round a fourth central core. The initial plans – such as they were – were to use a Saturn C-1, predecessor to the IB. The X-15 version would also be the X-15B, which was a two-crew orbital version of the plane. Neither

The assembled, but not painted upper stage for the Saturn IB, required to launch an X-15. A hole has been carefully drilled into the tip of the BPC to take the rear fuselage of the X-15.

The only conveniently available kit of the X-15 in 1:144 scale, the resin kit from Anigrand Craftswork.

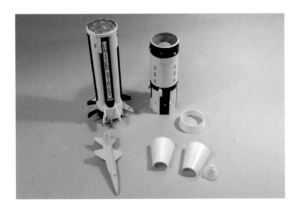

The assembled, but not finished, 1:144-scale X-15, with an already built Saturn IB, and the parts required from either that or another IB kit: the two-part SLA, lower ring and conical BPC that protects the Apollo command module during launch.

The X-15, now painted black, with the decals added, on top of the new adaptor section, now painted gloss white with some decals applied.

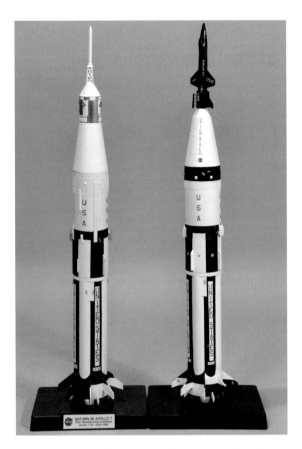

The X-15-launching Saturn IB, compared to the Saturn IB that launched Apollo 7.

1:175, 1:200 – but at that point, none in 1:144. In more recent years this was corrected as Dragon issued several that were actually in 1:144, but their availability was spasmodic, to say the least, and they were soon discontinued and became unobtainable.

Dragon made ready-built versions as well, using metal as well as plastic. However, this was never clear as, somewhat perversely, Dragon managed to issue catalogues and other advertising materials without saying precisely what is listed – is it a kit or is it a ready-built? But the scale was at least noted, and is 1:144, so at least you have some starting point.

In addition there have been two other options. This is definitely not a construction kit, but Corgi made a die-cast B-52 carrier aircraft and X-15 set-up, and that is in 1:144 scale. Finally – and for those who didn't mind building resin kits – there was one in resin from Anigrand Craftswork. However, even this wasn't straightforward, as it only came as a bonus to the kit of the Boeing XB-59, kit number AA-4059. As well as the XB-59, there are three 'bonus' kits in the box, one of which is the X-15. Incidentally – and to add to the total confusion when it comes to 1:144-scale versions of the X-15 – the box does not advertise any of these 'bonus' kits, it just appears you get the Boeing XB-59!

But – and assuming a 1:144-scale X-15 can be sourced – all the conversion parts for the Saturn IB can come from the IB kit. Besides the first and second stages you need the conical SLA – Spacecraft Lunar Adaptor – and the BPC – Boost Protector Cover – that goes over the Command Module (CM). The latter need the lugs where the LES (Launch Escape System) tower attaches removed, and any resulting holes filled, and the whole lot sanded smooth. Actually most of the tip of this part then needs removing, leaving the hole were the engine nacelle of the X-15 will sit.

Enlarge the hole with a round file until the X-15 engine part fits snugly. Strictly speaking this should be the X-15A-2 version with the External Tanks, as this would have been the only version actually built

the C-1 nor the X-15B were ever built, but the basis for the launcher would effectively have been the 'IB' set-up, so a Saturn IB can be the starting point. If a Saturn IB was used, the X-15 would sit vertically on the nose of an adapted upper stage, itself on top of the S-IVB stage and the S-IB first stage.

However, although the conversion can use the Airfix Saturn IB, there is a slight problem with an X-15. Although there are many kits of the X-15, oddly there is no conventional (that is, injection styrene) kit of the craft in 1:144 scale. There are a number of kits in the established aircraft scales of 1:32, 1:48 and 1:72, and there have been a number of other X-15 kits. For many years they came in at a wide variety of smaller scales – such as 1:100, 1:120, 1:125,

All three Saturn IB conversions from this chapter, left to right: the booster-augmented IB; the IB with a Centaur upper stage; and the X-15-launching IB. All sit on the conventional rectangular base that comes with both Airfix Saturn IB and V kits.

that would have been capable of reaching orbit. (There would still have been a problem with thermal protection for re-entry, but that will have to be put on one side for the moment.) Actually, if you can locate the Dragon 1:144-scale kits, one was of the X-15A-2 version.

These converted parts from the Saturn IB kit can be sprayed semi-gloss white, and maybe add some decals from the spares. Here a NASA meatball was used and a small 'UNITED STATES'.

The X-15A-2 was actually 29in (740mm) longer than the original, though this is not really noticeable in 1:144 scale; however, there should be the two external tanks that are certainly visible. So there is the option of scratch-building these two tanks, or just leave the X-15 'as is' – it was never flown this way after all.

CHAPTER 7

HEAVY LIFT SATURN V

In January 1963, NASA described a scientific space station known as the Large Orbiting Research Laboratory (LORL) that it wanted to have in orbit by 1970, serving as a manned base and a place from which to repair and service satellites already in space. To support future requirements for heavier payloads, internal studies began at NASA's Marshall Space Flight Center on bigger and more powerful variants of Saturn V.

Despite the trimmed-down magnitude of the basic Apollo Moon landing programme, NASA pressed ahead with studies for a future beyond the first landing, and it also began to define in more detail the kind of space station it wanted. LORL evolved into the more descriptive Manned Orbital Research Laboratory (MORL), launched by two Saturn V rockets and assembled in orbit as a rotating workshop for creating partial gravity from inverse centripetal force.

Seeing the Moon missions and the Earth-orbiting space station as two concurrent activities, NASA gathered this collective activity into the Apollo Applications Program (AAP), embracing both with a common set of hardware. It anticipated that the AAP would initially involve planning for three orbiting 'workshops' converted from redundant S-IVB rocket stages, three larger laboratories launched by separate Saturn Vs and four Apollo telescope mounts for observing the sun.

As the design centre for the Saturn rockets, the Marshall Space Flight Center wanted to provide an evolving series of launchers based on the Saturn V to accommodate all these expanding requirements. In March 1964 it issued a report on initial conclusions, defining six separate configurations.

Stating rather optimistically that 'it will become the "workhorse" of the 1970s', the first improvement, configuration A, would uprate the F-1 thrust output by 8 per cent to provide a net payload capability of 256,450lb (116,324kg). The third stage would incorporate an uprated J-2 engine to improve payload by a further 2,500lb (1,134kg). Configuration B would add propellant to the S-IC first stage, retain the same second and third stages as the baseline, and increase capacity to 267,000lb (121,110kg).

And so it went on, with configuration C increasing F-1 thrust by 20 per cent with significant changes to S-II and S-IVB mixture ratios and chamber pressures. Configuration D adopted that S-IC upgrade and replaced the five J-2 engines with a single cryogenic engine delivering 50 per cent more thrust than a standard S-II stage. Configurations E and F replaced the five F-1s in the S-IC with a plug-nozzle engine delivering a thrust of 9 million lb (40,032kN), the latter having strengthened S-IC and S-II stages to accept a nuclear-powered third stage. Each configuration could be augmented with solid boosters, but even without these the payload would increase to 405,320lb (183,853kg) or 151,419lb (68,683kg) to the Moon.

Between June 1964 and April 1965 a further eight studies were conducted for detailed analysis of what was now termed the 'modified launch vehicle'

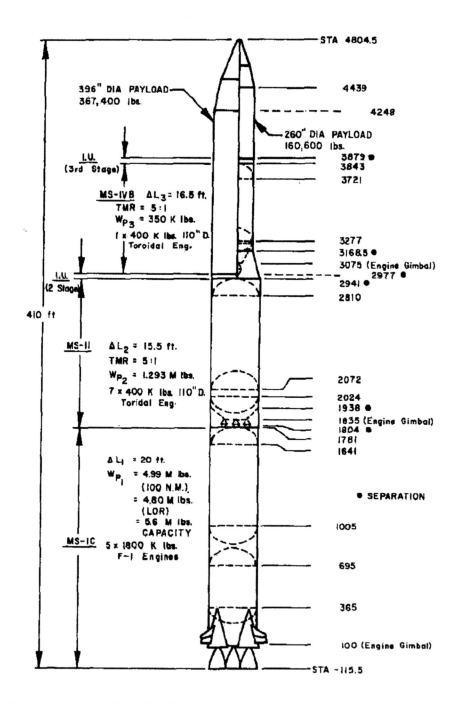

Carrying the prefix 'M' for Modified, an early proposal extended the length of each stage to increase the burn time and replaced the J-2s with a toroidal engine, raising payload to 367,000lb (166,471kg) and height to 410ft (125m).

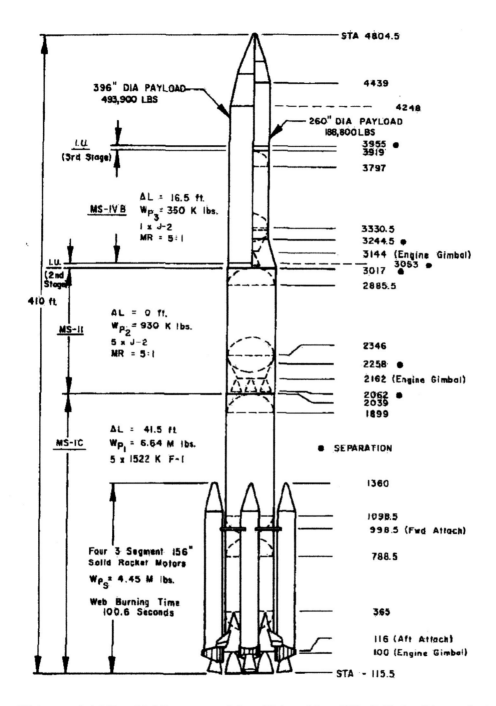

With extended S-IC and S-IVB stages, and the addition of four 156in (3.96m) solid propellant boosters, payload for this heavy-lift cargo version would have increased to 493,000lb (223,625kg).

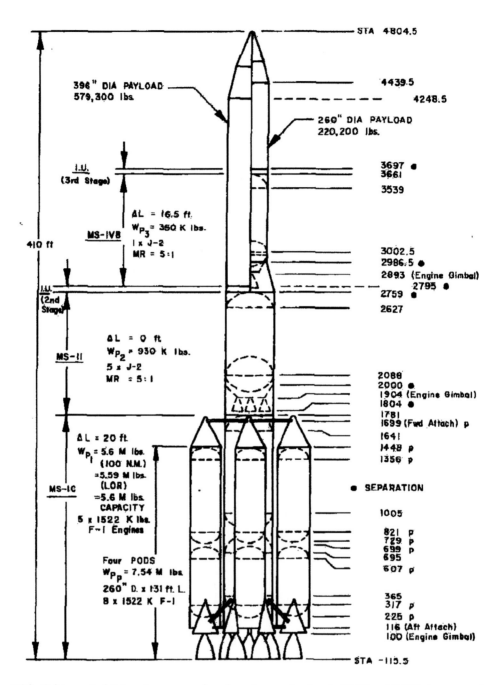

With eight uprated F-1 motors across four boosters and extended S-IC and S-IVB stages, payload reaches 579,300lb (262,770kg), more than twice the capacity of the standard Saturn V.

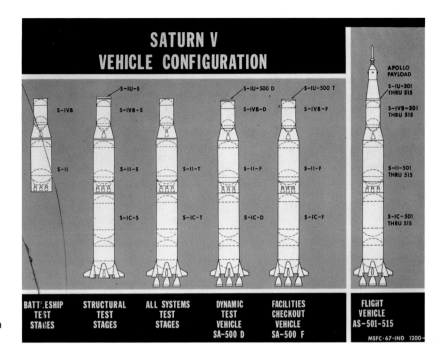

Saturn V configurations, including test vehicles and the standard Apollo-Saturn flight arrangement.

(MLV). The proposed options could have been applied following the fifteen Saturn Vs already under contract. Further analysis was necessary to refine the earlier studies and to keep pace with a changing structure to the future plan. As major spending on Apollo reached a peak, there appeared to be little chance of getting the ambitious programme desired.

Boeing did the next major analysis in early 1966, examining a shortlist of potential upgrades. In summary, category 1 was represented by a family of two stages with S-IC, equipped with three, four or five F-1s and a standard S-IVB, and known as the MLV-SAT-INT-20. Category 2, designated MLV-SAT-INT-21, comprised a two-stage vehicle with S-IC and S-II stages. Payload capacity for the Int-20 was 132,000lb (59,875kg) and 255,000lb (115,668kg) for Int-21.

Category 3 offered the same S-IC and F-1 options but with uprated engines in all three stages, known as the MLV-SAT-V-3B. With a height of 409.9ft (124.9m) and the more powerful uprated F-1s, the -3B would have had a payload capability of 367,400lb (166,652kg). In parallel, North American had studied an adaptation of the -3B known as the Int-17: this would have had S-II and S-IVB stages for a ground launch and an LEO (Low Earth Orbit) payload of 136,000lb (61,689kg).

Any further development would require new pad structures and infrastructure, potentially located at the initial locations for LC-39C and LC-39D, but never built. The study was limited to growth versions with LEO payload potential up to 960,000lb (435,456kg), but beyond little more than half that value a completely new assembly, handling and launch facility would have been required.

To accommodate the larger derivatives, especially those with strap-on solid or liquid propellant boosters, both launch pad and flame trench would need upgrades, together with new crawler transporter and mobile service structures. The boosted evolutions were assessed to be ready for flight from 1973.

Two years after the Boeing report, the Marshall Space Flight Center issued the definitive overview of possible upgrades with the Int-17 included, as was an -18.5, differing in having two 120in (304.8cm) solids and an LEO payload of 114,000lb (51,710kg). The -18.7 variant swapped from five- to seven-segment solids, increasing LEO capability to 145,000lb (65,772kg).

One unlikely proposal was to modify the base of the S-IC first stage into an S-1D in which the four outer F-1 engines and a thrust skirt would be jettisoned during ascent, leaving the central F-1 to place 50,000lb (22,680kg) in LEO.

The end of the Saturn V development effort came with a memorandum from NASA boss James Webb dated 31 August 1968, cancelling all future manufacturing and development work on different variants.

MODELLING AN EVEN LARGER SATURN V

Until the Project Artemis SLS rocket and SpaceX's Starship flew in recent years, the Saturn V rocket was the most powerful launch rocket that ever (successfully) lifted off from the surface of the Earth. And it retained this record for decades. The Soviet Union would have beaten this with its slightly more powerful N-1 Moon rocket, but that never got off

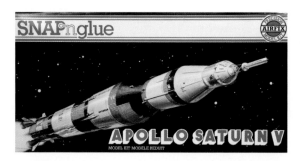

The first box for the Airfix Saturn V, where it had been converted to 'snap-n-glue'.

The original Airfix kit of the Apollo Saturn V.

The most recent box for the Airfix Saturn V. The 'snap' name is omitted, but the parts still have this option.

the ground. (To be absolutely correct, technically it did, but all four flights failed to get much altitude – if any, and one absolutely none at all as it exploded on the pad, taking not only itself out, but another N-1

Monogram's first issue of its 1:144-scale Apollo Saturn V. This kit is still available, though now under the Revell name.

and most of the launch site. So the N-1, intriguing launcher that it was – or could have been – does not exactly count.)

Consequently, due to its power and versatility it is not surprising that over the years there were many suggestions for upgrades and follow-on launchers based around the Saturn V being considered.

Being based on the Saturn V, it probably goes without saying that the starting point is a kit of the Saturn V. Although there are some in smaller scales, the main range starts at 1:200 scale from AMT, available in both its 'Man in Space' set (all five of the American crewed launchers at that time in one box, still the only kit to provide this), and the Saturn V was also issued, by itself, as a separate kit. It then progresses through 1:144-scale versions from both Airfix and Monogram (the latter now re-boxed as Revell, though the parts are identical), up to Revell's own originated 1:96-scale kit, and finally the largest (static) kit to date, the monster from Dragon in 1:72 scale. There are others produced as scale flying rockets, but these are really a subject in their own right and – in general – not suitable for these sorts of conversions, though it could be interesting to try!

So take your choice, though for convenience, and because of practicalities such as size constraints, plus given that at least two Saturn V kits will be needed for most conversions, the best compromise

is likely to be one of the 1:144-scale offerings. For most details the Airfix kit is used here, though the Monogram-Revell one is very similar, and could equally take pride of place.

The F-1 Engines

All these advance designs began at the lowest level, with the basic Saturn V S-IC stage with its five F-1 engines – though above that it appeared anything could go. There were a whole range of these proposals, some using larger upper stages and some using additional booster rockets for the S-IC first stage. So this conversion can frankly take a variety of routes depending on what you like the look of – and what you may have handy in the spares box.

So starting with the S-IC stage, both Airfix and Monogram have this engine stage as a plate that holds the F-1 engines and the five engine bells, each in two halves. The Monogram kit has always been a 'glue together' kit, but way back in 1980 the Airfix kit, having first been issued in 1969 as a conventional all-glue construction kit, was converted to a 'snap and glue' kit, where many parts could be snapped together without glue (though they can, of course, also be glued).

Snap kits have been around ever since there have been construction kits, but they were usually

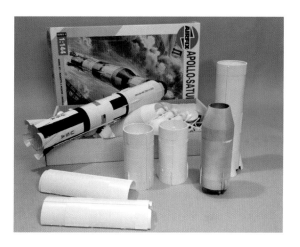

Sorting out some parts of the Airfix Saturn V that could be used.

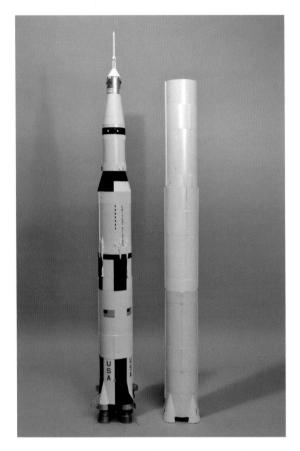

Testing out the sort of height that could be achieved. It is compared here with an Apollo Saturn V.

More of the range of parts, including some payload shroud options, and the boosters from the Heller Ariane 4 kit.

designed from the ground up as completely snap. Here there was a compromise, as the Saturn V did not start this way, so the 'snap and glue' label was introduced as some small parts still had to be glued. So it does make the whole reasoning as to why it was converted so that some were 'snap' slightly odd. However, the F-1 engine bells were converted to 'snap' to help hold them together while the cement dried. Incidentally – and this applies to any Saturn V kit – although the engine bells and support structure are 'metallic', the actual engine plate isn't – it's gloss white. Presumably this would also apply to whatever was the new proposal for a second-generation Saturn V.

With the basis of the S-IC stage, it is now time to decide what goes on top. Most proposals fell under increasing the launcher's height, and/or whether the first stage was fitted with additional booster rockets. Even these boosters varied widely, including solid fuel and liquid fuel versions of various sizes, and either fitted as pairs, or as four.

Where the height of the Saturn V is increased, many designs don't have a truncated stage – as occurs in the Apollo Saturn V, where the move from the second stage of the Apollo Saturn, the S-II, to the third, the S-IVB, uses a conical interstage. This was to change the width of the second stage to the thinner, S-IVB third stage. Consequently, these new proposals did change the look of the launcher considerably as they all went 'straight up' from the S-IC as far as the payload shroud.

This new look was emphasised as most of these proposals stood at least the height of the Apollo Saturn V, and some are even taller. They all appeared to be based on a standard S-IC stage as the first, and a S-II as the second, with a third stage, possibly another S-II, topped with the payload, likely with its own propulsion system. That was probably about the tallest rocket you could build in practice, given Saturn technology, so was the one that was decided upon here.

Building the Boosters

To get the height it was decided basically to put one S-IC stage on top of another, followed by the S-II, and then a final stage. Boosters are also going to be added, so this involves modifying the first stage,

the S-IC. The easiest source for boosters, without completely scratch-building, comes from the Heller kit of the Ariane 4 launcher (as used in the Saturn IB conversions, *see* Chapter 6). This is 1:125 scale, and has been issued under three different kit names: first was as 'Bobcat', in 1983; second as 'Bobkit', in 1986; and in 1990 it was reissued under Heller's own name.

Box-art, and whether it included the semblance of the launch pad, varied, but the main plastic

Close-up of the Ariane 4 liquid boosters. Each is very simply two parts, and these snap together.

Holding up one of the Ariane 4 boosters against the S-1C stage to mark the positions for the attachment lugs.

A slot is cut in the lower edge of the S-IC stage, indicated by the needle file, and a slot cut. Note here that slots also need to be cut in the F-1 engine bulkhead.

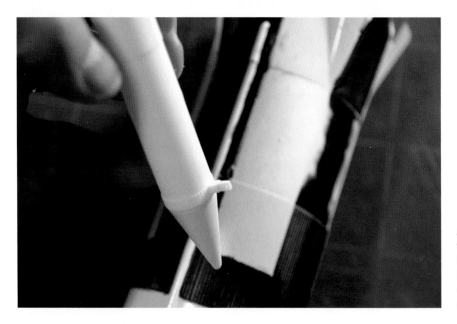

A slot is also drilled out for the upper booster lug. These are just below where the upper corrugated section starts on the S-IC stage.

parts were all the same. This version was the four liquid-fuelled booster version of the Ariane 4 (the Ariane 4L), so you get naturally four liquid-fuelled boosters. These are very simply two halves (and are also snap together – here the whole kit was designed as 'snap'), with locating pegs top and bottom on each. These pegs are used here to attach the boosters to the sides of the Saturn V S-IC stage.

Without the engine base plate in position, cut or file a slot in the bottom edge of the stage, centrally between the skirts. This will take the boosters' lower lug. Note that a corresponding slot needs to be cut out of the engine plate, before it is fitted in place.

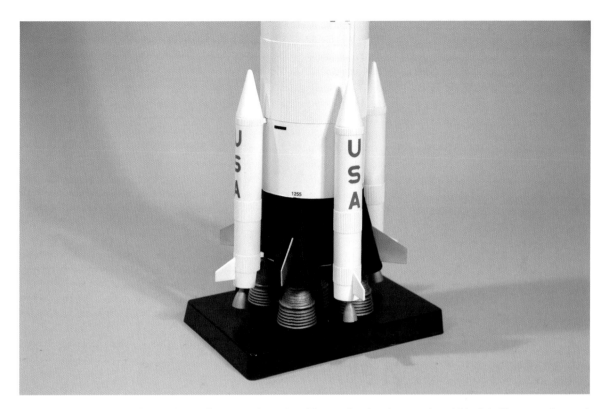

The completed S-IC stage for this 'tall' conversion. The skirt section has been painted black halfway up, instead of the alternating patterns, and 'USA' decals added to the boosters.

Repeat for all four sides. Next, offer a booster to the side of the S-IC stage, and you will see that – conveniently – the upper lug corresponds to just below the upper corrugated section.

Ensuring that the line is dead centre between the fin skirts and vertical from the lower lug, cut a corresponding slot. The easier way is to drill two small holes, one above the other the approximate width of the lug, and file them together as a slot. The boosters' lugs are 'T' shaped – the top bar of the T is intended to fit inside the rocket shell. This works for the lower lug, but the upper will need this 'top bar' cut away, so the upright of the T can fit though the slot – but these will hold in place in the finished models as they will eventually be glued in place.

The fitting of the boosters and the S-IC stage engine plate can now wait until the rest is constructed.

Gaining Height

To gain height, frankly the best option is to use another S-IC stage as the 'second stage'. It is not precisely the way the 'proposals' seemed to plan it – but these were 'proposals'. Here, the kit interstage was put on top of the lower S-IC stage, and the 'upper' S-IC modified at its lower edge to fit the upper part of the interstage. As both Airfix and Monogram kits have the lowest engine section with skirts and fins as a separate part, this means it doesn't need to be cut off – and the bottom diameter is identical to the top diameter of the S-IC stage. What does need altering is the way it is attached, but the original connecting lugs can be trimmed so the bottom edge fits the top edge of the interstage.

The S-II stage then fits the top of the second S-IC stage, as it would anyway. Here, though, the conical

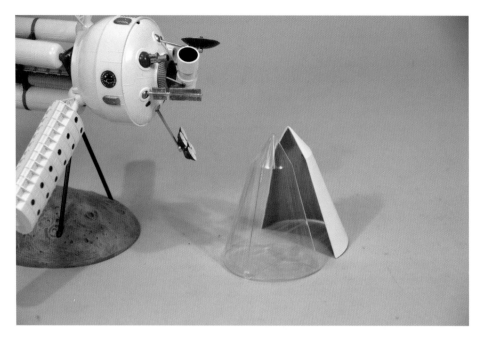

The source of the payload shroud for the very top, here taken from the MPC Pilgrim Observer kit. The shroud is supplied in two halves, one in clear styrene, one in the white of the kit. This conversion actually used two clear halves (from two kits), though the procedure either way is identical.

Placing the Pilgrim Observer shroud on top of the upper stage, and marking round it with a marker pen.

interstage section will need removing, and a new payload shroud made to fit. The one that comes with the Airfix Skylab Saturn V is too narrow (it fits the smaller diameter S-IV Stage, not the S-II stage), although the one from the Dragon Skylab Saturn V, as it is large scale at 1:72, could be adapted – though this is an expensive option.

Slightly cheaper is to use the fairing from the MPC kit of the Pilgrim Observer, and because this fairing does not have to be used to make the main Pilgrim

Sawing off the excess edge with a razor saw – care is required as clear styrene is 'raw' and more brittle than styrene, where rubber and colour pigment have been added.

Sanding the cut edge of the shroud on the sanding board.

Observer kit, you may well have these parts in the bits and pieces box. The kit was originally issued in 1970, but was long out of production and became very rare, and would not be recommended. But it was reissued in a new box in 2010, which makes availability easier. Besides the space station itself, it contained the fairing so it could be launched on a Saturn V. The kit was nominally 1:100 scale (presumably intended to sit atop the Revell 1:96-scale Saturn V), and so its fairing is marginally wider than

Attaching the modified shroud to the upper stage – note that a thin strip of plastic has been added to the upper stage, to aid the location.

the 1:144-scale Saturn. Cement the two halves of this fairing together (one half is moulded in clear), place it on top of the S-II stage, and mark the line to be cut with a marker pen.

Note that care needs to be taken cutting clear styrene parts as they are raw polystyrene, and raw polystyrene is far more brittle than coloured, which has colour pigment and also a small percentage of rubber added (which is why it is termed 'high impact polystyrene'). But with a fine razor saw and some care, clear styrene can be cut successfully.

We are not adding a payload here, though it could be an option, so the cut Pilgrim Observer shroud can be cemented directly on top of the S-II stage, any gaps filled, and sanded smooth.

The Final Finish

The final finish is really speculation, as it is with all these conversions. Production Saturn Vs had their distinctive black-on-white finish, the black

for temperature regulation and roll patterns, and these can be duplicated here, or a different scheme chosen.

One point always to watch when painting the black areas on Saturn V rockets is that many areas are corrugated, and getting masking tape to sit snugly over these is not easy – and ensure you use a good quality tape intended for model-making, not household sticky tape. Vertical masking is somewhat easier as you are following a line, but horizontal masking is harder because the tape is having to go continuously 'up and down' over the bumps! There is flexible model masking tape made that could be more suitable here, or even a material such as Blu-Tack can be used successfully, as it can be moulded into the indentations. (However, don't use Plasticine or its imitators, because although it is a popular modelling clay, the paint never dries on it, whereas it does on Blu-Tack!)

A way round this is to use either black decal sheet for all the 'black' areas, or – as a midway compromise

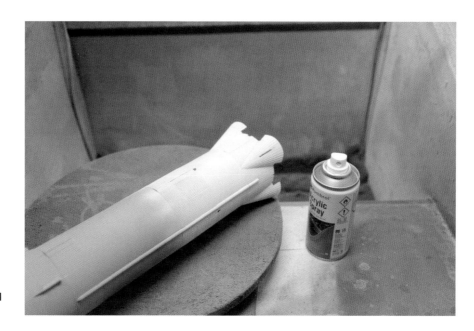

Painting any Saturn V starts with a good coat of white primer, here from the Humbrol range.

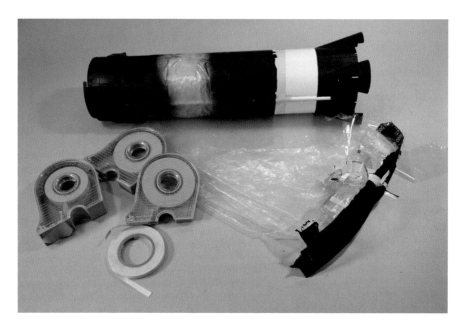

With any masking, a good quality masking tape is vital. Here the yellow tape is Tamiya. Old polybags (maybe the ones that come in the kits) can be recycled to mask wider sections.

– mask and paint as above, and then use thin black decal strip to 'emphasise' the edges and hide any imperfections.

With the stages completed, the boosters can be painted the usual gloss white, with metallic nozzles, and fitted to the first stage. The engine plate with the F-1 can then be fitted in afterwards. This will hold the lower booster lugs in place, though the upper will need cementing.

The final display can, of course, use the standard Airfix rectangular base – this is, after all, designed to fit the base of the Saturn V.

Removing the masking tape, here over the corrugated section of a Saturn S-II stage. Considering the multitude of indentations, this hasn't come out too badly!

All the parts for this extended Saturn V conversion, left to right: first stage, with boosters; second stage another S-IC stage; third stage, an S-II stage with the payload shroud.

The completed extended Saturn V, next to the Airfix Skylab Saturn V for comparison.

CHAPTER 8

SHUTTLE ON A SATURN

In 1969 President Nixon asked NASA to define a future that could take advantage of all that had been achieved to date while significantly reducing the agency budget and maintaining a dominant role in global space activities. The report identified a twelve-man space station as the immediate post-Apollo goal, with growth to a 100-man facility for orbital research in science and technology. To supply the station and continue to replenish it with logistical supplies and experiments, a reusable shuttlecraft was proposed as the core to achieving that at minimal cost.

In May 1970 NASA contracted North American Rockwell (NAR) and McDonnell Douglas for Phase B definition studies. The baseline configuration was for an Orbiter carried on the back of a booster but launched vertically. Taking the NAR design as representative, the fully reusable shuttle was big, with a lift-off weight of more than 5 million lb (2.26 million kg). The Orbiter would have a length of 206ft (62.78m) and a wingspan of 107ft (32.6m). The booster would have a length of 269ft (82m) and a wingspan of 144ft (43.9m), and would stand 102ft (31m) tall on its tricycle landing gear. In the vertical position for launch, the stacked configuration would have a height of 290ft (88.4m) and carry a payload of 65,000lb (29,484kg).

Much of 1971 was spent seeking ways to reduce the size of the Orbiter and the booster. NASA wanted highly efficient cryogenic engines to power both vehicles, and it was this that pushed up both the complexity and the cost. Initial alternative options suggested moving the liquid hydrogen from inside the Orbiter and placing it in two over-wing tanks that could be jettisoned in orbit, significantly reducing the cost and size of the Orbiter. In a further weight-reduction concept, the liquid oxygen was moved externally as well. Both propellants would now have to be contained in a separate External Tank (ET) and fed to the engines in the rear of the Orbiter by interconnecting pipes.

When initially conceived, the fly-back booster would have been powered by twelve rocket motors for launch and turbojet engines for getting back to a runway after dropping off the Orbiter. With the adoption of the External Tank for all Orbiter propellant, the staging velocity of the booster was reduced from 6,647mph (10,698km/h) to 4,772mph (7,679km/h). Partnered with Grumman on one of the studies, Boeing had responsibility and naturally turned to the S-IC it had built for Saturn V as a ready-made answer.

The fully reusable shuttlecraft would have a weight of 798,500lb (362,200kg), whereas the downsized Orbiter would reduce that to 494,900lb (224,486kg). And with the reduced staging velocity, the booster would not have to carry thermal protection. As studies progressed, McDonnell Douglas showed a proposal where the staging velocity was

This artist's view of the baseline Shuttle Orbiter displays the broad width of the fuselage for internal hydrogen and oxygen propellant tanks.

When engineers moved the voluminous liquid hydrogen tanks from the Orbiter to overwing tanks it reduced the size of the booster as well.

Boeing worked the potential for an S-IC as the Shuttle booster into a recoverable stage, but was outvoted by the lower cost of a solid propellant booster.

In June 1971, NASA boss James Fletcher supported a phased approach whereby an initial shuttlecraft would be partially reusable, retaining the smaller Orbiter but adopting a more conventional booster that might or might not be recovered. The objective here was to slash development cost, get it approved, and defer development of a full-scale booster, promising further reductions in operating cost, for later.

This encouraged the search for liquid propellant rockets and solid propellant boosters for an interim solution. Boeing responded initially by proposing the S-IC stage with the External Tank above and the Orbiter attached to the side of the ET. With a thrust of 7.5 million lb (33,360kN), the Saturn V first stage alone was capable of lifting the upper elements to a ballistic trajectory. But the evolved F-1 as studied for uprated versions of the Saturn V would increase that to 9 million lb (40,032kN) and absorb any weight growth or enhanced payload requirements.

There were other candidates, the nearest being the proposed Titan IIIL that required development of a new and larger core stage, but with six 120in (303.8cm) Solid Rocket Boosters (SRBs). When available, this promised a launch cost of $30 million compared with $73 million for the S-IC. But overall, because it was available, across 30 flights the total cost for a Shuttle based on the S-IC would come out even.

Boeing went even further and, carried away by the possibility, completed a highly detailed design for a manned fly-back S-IC stage equipped with wings, a separate tail unit, strengthened skin, a flight deck for two pilots, ten turbojet engines and a deployable landing gear. Overall, there would have been many problems in using the S-IC, but it was an equally valid candidate among an embarrassment of riches, the Marshall Center even proposing development of a completely new, pressure-fed booster for Shuttle and other applications.

a mere 4,227mph (6,802km/h), and that allowed a booster to be made from heat-sink materials alone, rather than complex thermal insulation required for the Orbiter.

MODELLING A SHUTTLE ON A SATURN

This could be one of the most intriguing Lost Projects, using elements of both NASA major crewed projects: Apollo and the Space Shuttle.

With the idea of lifting a Space Shuttle Orbiter to orbit using the S-IC stage of the Saturn V, this is a convenient build as kits of both the Saturn V and the Space Shuttle are available. Two are in the main 'space launcher' scale of 1:144, being Airfix for both kits and the combined Revell Shuttle and Monogram (now available under the Revell name) of the Saturn V. This build uses Airfix kits, though the Revell could be used, and in fact there is no reason why there cannot be a mix-and-match using both manufacturers.

There are few images of what this proposal could have looked like, and the main one appears as a model, though there is no indication of scale. It may even have been built from the commercial kits, though the NASA Model Shop did tend to do its own thing and build these sorts of exhibition models from scratch.

Here, though, we are using commercial kits, and from the Saturn V kit the only section required is the S-IC stage, though with the conical reduced section from the top of the S-II stage. The first task is therefore carefully to cut this conical section from the S-II stage, and there is the choice of either doing it while the section remains as 'halves', or with them cemented together.

Both methods have pros and cons. Cutting them before joining means the halves can be laid flat on the work surface, which could make for easier cutting. But there could be mismatches, which is avoided if the halves are joined first. Either way some sanding of the lower edges could be necessary, in which case the ubiquitous sheet of sanding paper glued to a sheet of plywood is the best method as it ensures a regular flat edge.

The two halves of the existing S-IC stage will need the locating edge at the top removed, and the new cut conical section firmly cemented in place.

The start of the S-IC stage for this conversion needs the top connecting ring removed. Here with black marker-pen stripes, and compared with a built Apollo Saturn V S-IC stage top, where the join is painted yellow.

Similarly the conical interstage of the S-II stage needs sawing off.

The sawn edges of the rocket sections are cleaned up on the sanding pad.

Meanwhile the engine section can be assembled separately and built up as the plans depict, as there is no reason to assume the proposal would be any different to the one that launched Apollo. This can include painting the four fins and the lower edges of the fairings silver, or you may wish to leave them all white, as is invariably depicted in any industrial model of such proposals.

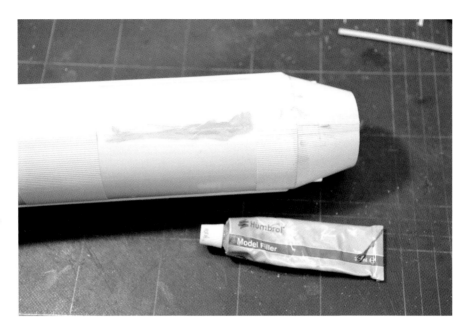

The conical interstage, from the S-II stage, is cemented to the top of the S-IC stage, and any gaps filled with one of the modelling fillers. The filling also applies to the vertical joins of the S-IC stage.

Rebuilding the New Second Stage

The only part requiring a complete rebuild is the new second stage, as this is in effect half a stage, to accommodate the Shuttle Orbiter. It could be possible to adapt the existing S-IVB stage, though you would need both halves, joining one on top of the other, then cutting down to one of approximately half its length – that is, you end up with a stage that is one-and-a-half times the height of an existing S-IVB stage. You then need to find a suitably shaped cone – or half a cone – to top the structure. Half the Spacecraft Lunar Adaptor (SLA) structure from the Saturn V was tried, but ended up somewhat too long.

The two S-IVB stages from the Apollo Saturn V are lined up against the length of an already built Orbiter. (Though not the one used in the finished model.)

The two S-IVB stage halves, compared to an assembled S-IVB stage.

The two halves of the S-IVB stage, joined lengthways, compared to the parts of the Skylab on the runner, as included in the Airfix Skylab Saturn V kit.

In fact it is easier to use the most recent adaptation of the Airfix Saturn V kit, that of the version that launched Skylab in 1973. Unfortunately there is no Monogram/ Revell equivalent, so if you are just using that kit, you will have to use the former suggestion of adapting the S-VIB stage.

The Airfix Skylab Saturn V also includes a suitable conical top section. If you use the Airfix Skylab 'S-IVB'

stage (which of course is actually Skylab), keep the lower section as a complete circle, as it will attach to the S-IC stage far more easily. Then angle a cut to the halfway point. Flat stock styrene sheet can then be fitted into the open section.

The Shuttle Orbiter used in the NASA-type exhibition models will invariably be of 'simplified' form, such as with no RCS (Reaction Control System)

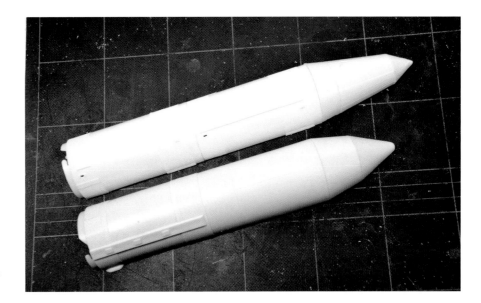

Two versions of the 'half' upper stage of this conversion. The top uses the S-IVB stage and the SLA stage from an Apollo Saturn V kit. Below is 'half' of the Skylab section from the Skylab Saturn V kit. It was decided to use the latter, as it works better.

Some of the detail on the Skylab stage can be removed using a sanding drum in an electric drill. However, this is optional for this conversion.

openings, leading edges or other 'details'. But unless you feel like 'retro-engineering' the existing Airfix, Revell, Minicraft or Dragon 1:144-scale Orbiters, it is probably best (and easier) to leave it as 'flightworthy'.

However, one conversion that will be necessary is the addition of two liquid-fuel tanks that can supply the existing Orbiter Space Shuttle Main Engines. These are positioned over each wing, attached – probably to the fuselage, as against the

wing – with attachments through which the fuel would pass. There are no details of the way these would attach, though here for the convenience of ensuring a model with 'strong' connections (unlike, for example, the way the SRBs are attached to the ET, which never looked strong enough in real life, let alone reduced to 1:144 scale), small-diameter EMA pipes were fitted through the Orbiter fuselage, and cut flush with the exterior surface.

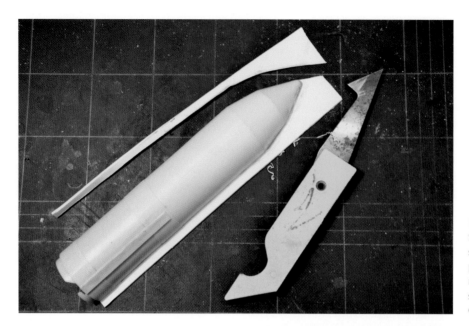

Laying the 'half' Skylab-based second stage on a sheet of plastic to cut out the main backing area that sits adjacent to the Orbiter.

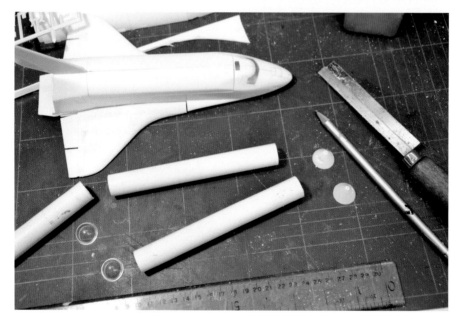

Cutting out the parts for the new fuel tanks that will fit each side of the Orbiter. The aft hemispheres are EMA parts; the forward cones are Apollo command modules.

The two fuel tanks were built from EMA tube, 6in (150mm) long. The exact diameter isn't clear, but tubing ¾in in diameter was used (VT-24). The aft end of each tank is finished with a matching diameter hemisphere, while the front end is conical. For that, the easiest source is to use the Command Module (CM) from the Saturn V kit, though you would need

two, with the various window recesses filled in and sanded smooth. These also need reducing in height, to reduce the base diameter, and sandpaper on board is the easiest method. Just keep checking that not too much plastic is being removed. A half-round strip was added on the outer side of the tube, and a flat strip on the inner.

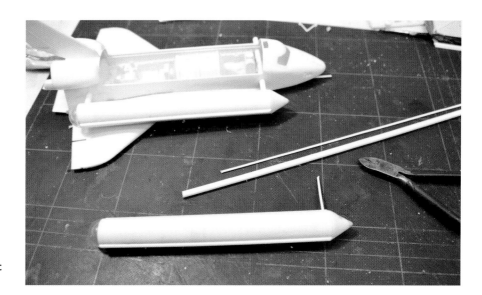

The fuel tanks are assembled and trimmed with flat and half-round plastic strips on each side.

The tanks were then marked up to line up with the holes in the Orbiter, more thin-diameter pipe was used as the main connector, and EMA P-2 (which is also classed as pipe, but is actually plastic-coated wire) fitted to the end, which will then slip into the pipe tubes built into the Orbiter. None of the details in this section is sacrosanct, and if you have pipe, tubes, hemispheres and cones of different origins and diameters, they can be adapted.

Attaching the Orbiter to the Saturn

At this point some method of attaching the Orbiter to the Saturn had to be devised, and the easiest is to use the parts that are actually used to attach it to the ET. First, note that the forward attachment point will need moving back by around 1in (25mm), otherwise it is above the top of the new second stage for the Orbiter. This is simply a matter of filling in the old location hole and drilling a new one, marking

The new upper stage is detailed with the support and attachment structure from the Space Shuttle kit. Note the lower section is retained as a complete circle as it will attach to the conical intersection far better than if it were purely a 'half' section.

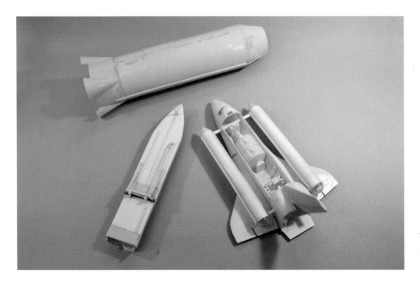

The main components of this conversion, primed but not otherwise painted.

out carefully where this will go on the new stage. At the same time, mark where the main attachment point holes are in the Orbiter, as this will have to correspond to the two rear attachment pipes.

The main attachment part is glued to the new stage, and as many, or as few, of the additional parts added. Frankly there is no point in using the very small pipes you get especially in the Airfix kit,

though the thicker pipe that attaches to the upper LOX (liquid oxygen) tank in the ET can be adapted to fit.

The Final Stage: Painting the Model

With the main construction done, it is time for the finish. The S-IB stage was completed more or less as

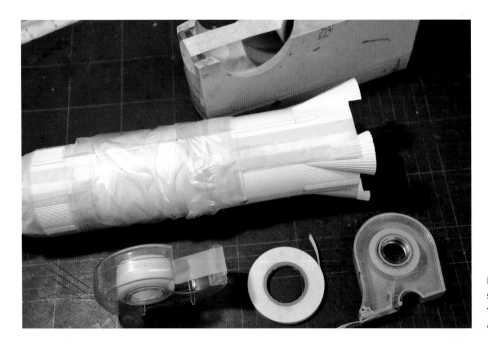

Masking the S-IC stage to produce the classic 'black and white' pattern.

Close-up of the masking for the vertical black 'stripes' on the lower section of the S-IC stage.

If paint seeps through when painting these corrugated sections, all is not lost. Here an old toothbrush dipped in acrylic thinner (the Humbrol satin black aerosol is acrylic) is being used to carefully wipe away the overspill. However, this will only work if the paint hasn't thoroughly dried.

it would have been for launching Apollo, or Skylab for that matter. First the whole structure was sprayed Humbrol gloss white, over matt white. Then once thoroughly dry, the areas for the roll-pattern black panels on the lower section were masked off, as were the upper equivalents. These were then spray-painted with Humbrol satin black over matt black.

When painting these sorts of patterns, especially where the kit has the corrugated 'stringers', you will be very unlikely not to get some 'creep' of paint,

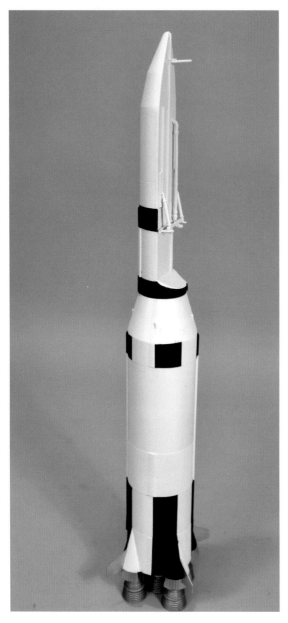

Test-fitting the completed new second stage on to the new upper stage on the conventional S-IC first stage.

old – but because this is so slight, it should not be discernible.)

However, if there are areas where paint has crept under the masking, first try and dab off the excess using a very thin amount of thinner on a cotton bud. This will usually work. If the area is larger, you could try using one of the modelling wax/polishes: because these are very slightly abrasive, they will 'sand' off the excess paint. In the worst case scenario it might mean lightly retouching in the 'other' colour, though this is best done when the paint is more thoroughly dried.

The new upper stage was painted similarly, but here – as it isn't detailed in the few existing art works – a band of black was applied to the lower corrugated section, and a similar band higher up.

New Fuel Tanks for the Orbiter

For the Orbiter, the new fuel tanks, which had at this point not been permanently fitted, were spray-painted gloss white. The main Orbiter was then also painted. Given that the kits are all 'production Orbiters', different colours and finishes were used to make them appear a little more 'prototype'. First the main Orbiter was painted semi-gloss white. As this is speculative, the individual panels of matt white found on production Orbiters were not applied. Early plans for the Orbiters had the undersides in light blue, not black, so here Testor's intermediate blue was used, with the demarcation lines between upper and lower finishes simplified, especially round the nose.

The rear engine bulkhead was also painted intermediate blue, while the main Space Shuttle Main Engine (SSME) bells were painted aluminium, and the smaller orbital engine bells in red, as often depicted in early artwork (though these were in fact covers over the bells). Red was also used for the RCS nozzle openings (again for the same reason – they were covers over the openings). The wing leading edges were painted aluminium, though in reality they were more the intermediate blue colour, while the cockpit glass was sprayed transparent blue.

however well it is masked. The secret is to get the masking removed as soon as the paint is touch dry. (This also helps to allow the two paints to 'blend' with an ever-so-slight flow of the new paint over the

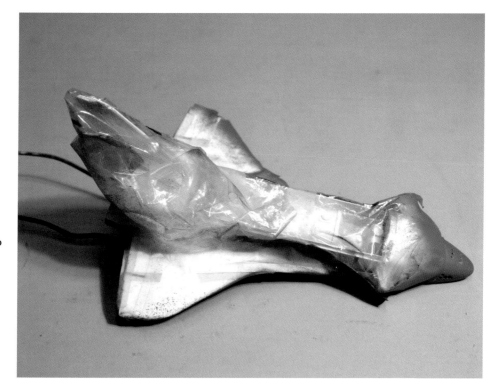

Masking the Orbiter, already painted white, so the intermediate blue can be sprayed on – this is primarily for the underside, but the nose – as visible here – is also finished in this colour.

With the Orbiter masking removed, a detail of the mounts for the new fuel tanks either side of the cargo bay can be seen. (Note the Spacelab payload is fitted – not that it is required, as the doors are finished closed – but its structure adds rigidity to the Airfix version of the Orbiter as a whole.)

125

The engine end of the Orbiter showing the paint scheme: the engine bulkhead is intermediate blue; the SSME bells dark aluminium and the OMS (Orbital Maneuvering System) bells are red.

Applying Decals

Finally, decals were applied. Using most from the existing kit decal sheets, the S-IB stage had USA and Stars and Stripes applied, more or less as they would have been for Apollo launches. The new upper stage had two of the original S-II stage red UNITED STATES applied, 90 degrees apart. The other two of these decals were applied to the two Orbiter new fuel tanks. These also had black detail lines applied round the top and bottom of each tank.

The Orbiter itself used NASA 'meatballs' from an aftermarket decal sheet, one large one applied on one wing, and small ones on each side of the fin – the latter was not used on mission Orbiters. The 'United States' and flag decals for the Orbiter sides were used, but moved position and were applied to the cargo-bay doors instead. As a tribute to the first Orbiter (and not forgetting *Star Trek*), the craft was named *Enterprise*.

Uniting the Stages and the Orbiter

Finally, the stages and the Orbiter were united. If the fit is close enough you will probably get away without gluing. The original kit base, especially from the Airfix Saturn V kit, could be used. The Monogram one is slightly more complex, though could be adapted.

Interestingly, this idea is almost replicated in Project Artemis. Yes, no actual Saturn V parts, and no Orbiter, but Artemis certainly combines elements of both Apollo and the Space Shuttle programmes.

Opposite: **The completed conversion of a Space Shuttle Orbiter being launched by a Saturn V first stage.**

CHAPTER 9

FLY-BACK BOOSTERS FOR THE SHUTTLE

A NASA study in 1975 sought to replace the Solid Rocket Boosters (SRBs) with a recoverable Liquid Rocket Booster (LRB), and increase the overall Orbiter payload capability. It examined four types of engine, including the existing Space Shuttle Main Engine (SSME), the F-1 and two versions of a new high-pressure motor, one with a thrust of 680,000lb (3,024kN) and another with a thrust of 800,000lb (3,558kN). Maximum payload capability across a wide range of options was 140,000lb (63,504kg).

Shortly after the Challenger disaster of 28 January 1986, plans were made to replace the SRBs with an Advanced Solid Rocket Motor (ASRM) with a diameter of 12.5ft (3.81m) and increased thrust to add 12,000lb (5,443kg) to the payload carrying capacity of the Orbiter. After development costs soared to $3.25 billion the programme was cancelled in 1993 when enhanced safety measures were applied to existing SRBs.

Liquids were the only sensible replacement option, and the most sought after was the Liquid Fly-Back Booster (LFBB). From the launch pad up it would fly

Launched on the thrust of fly-back Solid Rocket Boosters, a second-generation Shuttle is visualised as it might have appeared.

Fly-back boosters separate and return to Earth, leaving the Orbiter to achieve orbit on its SSMEs.

A wind-tunnel test model of the Shuttle with the catamaran configuration transforming two boosters into a single 'aeroplane'.

LFBB "catamaran" concept model
NASA Langley Research Center   3/20/1998   Image # EL–1998–00052

a normal SRB flight profile, fly back to the launch site, and land on a runway from where it would return to flight. The concept was not new, but the technology that did not exist when the SRBs were selected began to appear as the programme evolved.

The LFBB concept formally began with the start of a feasibility assessment in September 1994, and concluded that this was the only sensible replacement for the existing SRBs. For a while it appeared that development costs would be prohibitive, but it bounced back into popularity when a general drive began to put together a range of Shuttle modernisation upgrades, rather than abandon the programme for new deep-space objectives.

Two configurations were selected, either of which would meet all the requirements and achieve the desired objectives: two separate boosters, such as existing SRBs, or a catamaran arrangement in which the two boosters were permanently attached together by a linking wing section.

The dual concept envisaged four liquid-propellant engines in each booster with a length of 141.3ft (43m) and a tank diameter of 16.7ft (5.1m), a wing area of 2,184ft² (202.89m²), an empty weight of 206,881lb (93,841kg) and a lift-off weight of 1.342 million lb (608,731kg). Existing Shuttle SRBs had a height of 149.16ft (45.46m), a diameter of 12.17ft (3.71m) and a weight of 1.3 million lb (589,680kg).

The LFBB had four fly-back jet engines in the forward fuselage area with deployable inlets after re-entry. The design of the wing was flexible, but with a leading edge sweep of 35 degrees and location aft to avoid flow conflict with the Orbiter wings.

The catamaran concept also had four engines in each booster, a length of 143.9ft (43.86m) and a diameter of 17.8ft (5.42m). The span across the two wings was 120ft (36.57m), and the wing area was 4,210ft² (391.11m²) with a leading-edge sweep of 42 degrees. Dry weight would have been 401,654lb (182,190kg) with a lift-off weight of 2.669 million lb (1.21 million kg).

A decision as to which to build was never made because the concept was considered too expensive with minimal overall return – but the mission profile for the LFBB is a fascinating study in 'what might have been'.

The boost phase from launch to separation lasted 2min 10sec, and achieved a height of 149,508ft (45,750m) and a speed of 3,710mph (5,971km/h), or Mach 5. As the Orbiter and the ET continued to ascend, so too would the two spent boosters, reaching a maximum height of 254,999ft (77,723m), 1min 40sec later, at which point they would begin to descend under gravity. Entry would occur at an elapsed time of 5min 33sec, at a height of 125,000ft (38,100m) and a 40-degree angle of attack.

With lifting descent, at 7min 37sec, and a height of 37,353ft (11,385m) and an 8-degree angle of attack, the booster would decelerate through Mach 1. Four minutes later it would start an aerodynamic turn on to the proper heading, 249.7 miles (401.8km) from Kennedy Space Center (KSC), and at Mach 0.984 maintaining the 8-degree angle of attack. Completing the transonic manoeuvre, the jet engines would start at 7min 48sec, 248 miles (400km) out from KSC at a height of 31,000ft (9,449m) and Mach 0.85. The cruise home would take less than 48min, an auto-touchdown occurring at 55min 28sec and at a speed of 218.6mph (352km/h).

By 1997 the options had been examined and the LFBB concept was put on hold, as the advantages were just not deemed to be worth the effort. In 1989 a further study into replacing the SRBs with recoverable liquid-propellant boosters verified the advantages in having four engines in each one. A decade or so later, further consideration of improvements and upgrades were shelved, and the inevitable decision was made to retire the Shuttle.

MODELLING THE SHUTTLE WITH FLY-BACK BOOSTERS

When the Space Shuttle idea was being planned, initially it was assumed it would be fully reusable: a – somewhat obviously – crewed orbiting craft that would reach orbit, but also a crewed booster section, which when it had performed its task of boosting the Orbiter to its goal, would return to base, land, and be readied for its next carrier flight. This was the almost guaranteed way that things would go – there was no real reason to think otherwise. This was so much so that even as early as 1958, eminent space scientist Willy Ley, working with Monogram, designed two craft that would fulfil these plans: Monogram released these as the Passenger Rocket and the Orbital Rocket.

But this logical route wasn't to be, and the plans changed to what we knew as the STS – Space Transportation System – with the Orbiter that carried a crew, but with a booster section that was something of a compromise. Consequently, the aircraft-shaped Orbiter did, more or less, match what had been planned all along, but the boosters took on a completely different appearance. So we ended up with the giant External Tank, the ET, that would contain the cryogenic fuels of liquid oxygen and liquid hydrogen: these fuels would feed three SSMEs that were themselves attached to the Orbiter, and so would be recoverable.

But this was not all, because on each side of the ET stood two SRBs, the largest and most powerful solid-fuel rocket engines produced to date. On lift-off all five engines fired, the SRBs being jettisoned at 26 miles (42km) altitude, splashing down in the ocean to be recovered, refurbished and reused. The Orbiter, with the ET still attached as it was still providing fuel for the engines, continued to orbit, the ET being finally jettisoned at around 70 miles (113km) altitude, and left to re-enter and burn up in the atmosphere.

'Space – as it should have been': the ideal scenario for launching astronauts into space – crews in both the orbital section and the booster section. These space launchers were designed by Willy Ley and issued as 1:192-scale kits by Monogram in 1958.

Three Decades Of Missions

The STS missions lasted 30 years (the first flight STS-1 in 1981, the final flight STS135 in 2011), but in the intervening years there was no shortage of 'advanced plans'. One would be to – slightly – recapture the initial plan of a totally recoverable booster section, by fitting both SRBs – though by now they would be 'LRBs': Liquid-Fuelled Rocket Boosters – with wings, and the ability to return and land automatically.

Taking an existing Space Shuttle kit, a version of this set-up can be built – though depending on the way it is built, you could need the parts from up to six other Orbiters! So as with many cases throughout this book, there is perhaps a use for spare parts, the bits and pieces box, or already built kits that have seen 'better days'.

The new boosters built here are based around 1½in tube. An EMA part was used here (part number VT-150). However, similar sizes are available (and are far cheaper) as domestic waste pipes, usually white in colour, or even cardboard postal tubes that can be wrapped in thin plastic sheet. Whatever the source of the tube, it will need a nose cone. The kit SRBs are too narrow in diameter, so a new nose cone will have to be found or made. There are several options:

The initial set-up for the new 'fly-back' boosters: a length of EMA tube (top), and a selection of 1:144-scale Orbiter parts.

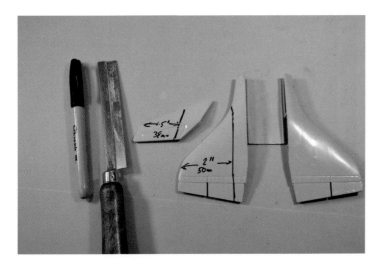

Preparing the wings for the new liquid-fuel fly-back boosters – here using the Airfix Orbiter kit. The wings have been marked with the dimensions for cutting, so all four wings will match. The same is done for the fin.

A selection of potential 'nose cones' for the new boosters. Top left: kit parts; centre and lower: EMA vac-formed shapes (the centre one of which was used for this build); top right: an alternative source – these are from ice-cream cones!

- Cones have been available as EMA vacuum-formed accessories (VC-500 and VC-605), though the availability of these could be difficult. However, two were used in this conversion.
- Cones are available in other space-rocket kits, the tops for the Heller Ariane 4 launcher for example, or even the top of the Shuttle ET, where the tops could be cut down to a suitable diameter. As this conversion does, in practice, require several Shuttle kits you could very well have ET parts in the spares box.
- Cones can be found in flying model rocket kits, and their accessory packs.
- Cones can also be got as spinners for flying model aircraft propellers.
- There could also be alternative sources, some not kit-based, so think laterally and look around. For example the vac-formed tops of some ice-cream cones are, well, conical booster-top shaped!

It is also relatively straightforward to cement a block of hard balsa wood into one end of the tube, using two-part resin or superglue, and sanding it into the cone shape. A mechanical sander is obviously the easiest here, and some can be bought reasonably cheaply, or accessories can be obtained that attach into an electric drill. Finish the balsa cone with sanding sealer, and it will be ready to paint, along with the standard plastic parts.

Some illustrations of this set-up appear to show what could be an actual Shuttle Orbiter nose, which could then suggest that these boosters were crewed, which was not the plan (in most cases). However, the rough diameter of the 1:144-scale Orbiter is about 1½in, so there could be the possibility of cutting the nose section and using that. As with the external tank parts, this conversion could supply some unused Orbiter nose sections, though a lot of cutting and filling would be needed, and it is probably not the recommended way to go.

Building the Wings

However a nose cone is sourced, the next task is the wings. The artwork that does exist indicates a similar shape and pattern to the actual wings of the Orbiter, so that was the route used here. If using the Airfix kit, the upper wing halves are separate, but the lower halves are moulded as one piece with the fuselage underside. The exact size – as with most of these conversions – is not vital, but as you need four wings (for two boosters), it could be an idea to mark out what sizes you are using on the first wing, just so you have a handy reminder when it comes to cutting the other three! The wings do appear to be of a smaller wingspan than the Orbiter equivalents; here they were cut halfway through the inner elevon, and at this point a straight cut was made.

133

The boosters also each have a fin and rudder, and again the one from the Orbiter was adapted. But again it appears shorter than the Orbiter version, so was cut at a height of 1½in (38mm). However, and this time unlike the Orbiter, these fly-back boosters have canard wings forwards towards the nose. If the plan for the shape of the main wings is somewhat vague, the canards are even more so. In some ways they resemble the fins/rudders of the Orbiter – and this is where the number of kits could come into play. If building these boosters with these suggestions, each booster will use two Orbiter wings and three Orbiter fins. As there are two boosters, this number doubles, hence the possible need for six Orbiter kits!

Using Revell kits, you can buy just the Orbiter, whereas the Airfix kit is only available as the full stack, so could be a (slightly) cheaper option. Even if you are using an Airfix kit as the original, the use of the Revell kit – or any of the other 1:144-scale Orbiter kits – for the fins is hardly going to matter. Here, even the main wings were made up from a mix of both Airfix and Revell kits – and the fit top and bottom from both companies was almost exact!

It helps that canards are usually a lot smaller than the main wings, and bearing in mind the fact that you need four, in the end the fin sections from an Airfix Saturn IB were cut off – there are eight in total – and these were used instead. Another

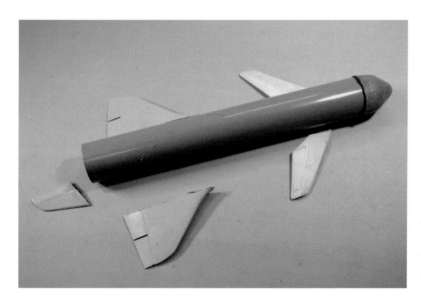

Test-fitting wings to the cut tube (that already has the nose cone attached). Here, the initial plan for using Orbiter fins as the canards was still in play.

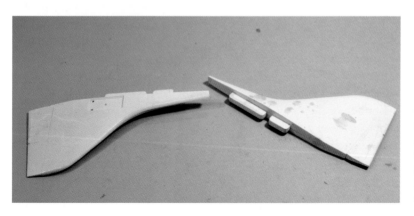

Comparing wings: left is the Airfix Orbiter wing, cut from the central underside section; right is the Revell, identifiable by the attachment lugs, which will be removed.

alternative is that aircraft kits could be suitable, and if wings are used, as against fins, you would only need two identical kits.

Attaching the Wings to the Booster Bodies

The main wings appear to be connected to the booster bodies in a similar position to that in a conventional aircraft (or the Shuttle Orbiter for that matter): thus they are not attached dead centre to the booster fuselage but lower down. This means sanding the edge of the new wings at such an angle that they can be glued to the tube, but still end up

Attaching the wings (the Airfix in this case) to one booster.

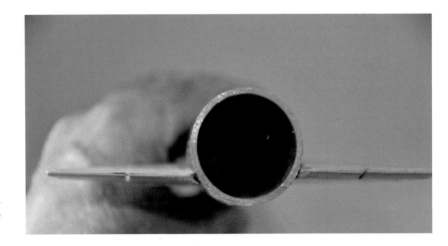

Ensure the two wings of each booster are lined up – frankly this is best done by eye.

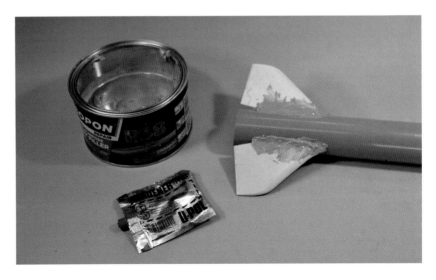

Applying filler – here, car-body repair filler – to the gaps that are bound to be seen over and under the wings.

135

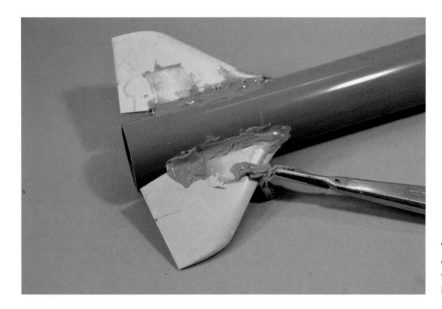

With the resin filler partially cured, it can be easily trimmed with a sharp knife, in this case a scalpel blade.

The two new booster basic assemblies. The canards are now replaced with the fins from the Saturn IB First Stage. The colours of the plastic of the main wings indicate that the grey (right) are all Airfix, while the left-hand ones are a mix of Airfix and Revell.

horizontal. This can be done with files and sanding, though a mechanical circular or band sander will be faster, as quite a considerable amount of plastic can be sanded off reasonably quickly. Though of course remember the fairly obvious point that sanding generates heat, and heat melts the plastic as well as 'tearing' it away, so do this with frequent pauses to remove the sanded/part-melted plastic – with care, as it will be hot!

Alternatively use the wings 'square' and block out the attachment with plastic sheet, or pre-formed square plastic strip.

Either way it is very unlikely that you will get an exact match to the circular body tube, but you need enough of a surface so that it can be initially cemented in place. Carefully ensure both wings are in the same position relative to the tube, and are horizontal to one another. However good the cutting and sanding, there will be gaps, probably on both upper and lower surfaces.

When the cement is dry and the wings firmly attached, ideally first fill these gaps with resin filler (the type used for car body repairs). This uses a catalyst (usually red) to speed up curing the resin (usually grey), and thorough mixing will result in a dark pinkish colour. But don't wait too long as these resins cure very quickly – and the more catalyst, the faster the curing time, and the hotter it can get – so use sparingly.

These resin filler kits come with spreaders and mixers, though these are really too large for the type of modelling work needed here. Plastic knives would be ideal but, due to sustainability issues, these are becoming unobtainable. Alternatively, use an old metal knife or artist pallet knife. However, you would need to carefully wipe clean any excess resin before it cures.

Because the resin cures chemically, you can apply fairly thick coats, so here it will easily fill the gaps left from cementing the wings in place. However, it is extremely unlikely you will get it completely filled and smooth in one take. Usually it is best to over-fill, and once the resin has cured so it is hard – that is, it will no longer flow – it is nevertheless still soft enough to start to trim using a sharp scalpel blade. Once this is done and the resin has thoroughly hardened, it can be sanded.

Wet-and-dry sanding is best for resins, and using this method you will soon end up with a smooth surface. But it is still very unlikely to be completely flush with the surface of the model. Any large holes, gaps or recesses can be refilled with more resin, but if it is a purely shallow recess, use standard model putty – having ensured that the surface is thoroughly dry from the wet-and-dry sanding.

Model putty dries by evaporation, so keep the layers thin – you can always do this several times – and once that is dry, more wet-and-dry sanding should bring the surface to its final smooth finish, fully blended in with the plastic. Remember the touch of a finger is more of an indication as to the finish than the eye. Once satisfied with the overall finish, then spray with primer, and that will also show up any remaining imperfections.

With the main wings in position, the tail fin can be added – here it is less likely to need filling, but a touch may be necessary. The forward canard wings can be added next, and these could be set central to the booster body. Canards on aircraft are invariably set higher than the main wings. Some filler might be needed with these, but almost certainly far less than the main wings, and ordinary modelling filler/putty is probably all that is required.

Sourcing the Engines

The boosters of course need engines, and the few illustrations there are, all vary. It appears that up to six (maybe eight?) could have been proposed. One source for these could be the Airfix Saturn IB, which has eight Rocketdyne H-1 engines. The Saturn IB engine plate that holds the engines is too

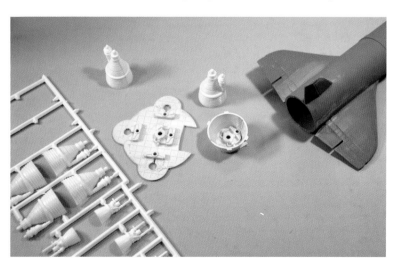

The rocket engine is an F-1 from an Airfix Saturn V. Its attachment plate is sawn from the Saturn bulkhead and trimmed to fit the SRB skirt.

The liquid-fuelled booster 'F-1' engine being test-fitted in place.

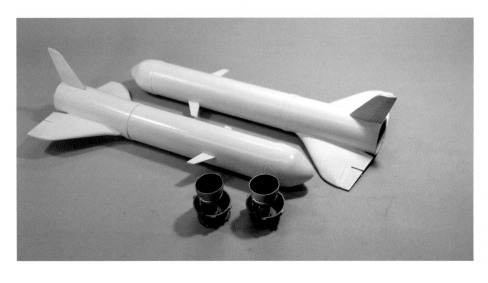

The new boosters are painted white, and the rocket engine metallic shades.

wide for our new booster, but could be cut down. Alternatively, the inner four could be used, omitting the outer four, or making a new plate completely and drilling the holes for as many as you feel necessary – four, five, six or eight could be the recommended numbers.

However, an alternative, which would more than match the SRB engine set-up, would be to use just one. This could be such as one of the Saturn V S-1B first stage engines – the F-1. These are about the size

of the original SRB solid-fuel nozzles. As an engine plate, the ends of the original SRBs – the 'skirt' section – can be cut off, turned upside down and have the hold-down lugs filed down so they fit up inside the new tube. Then the engine plate for the Saturn V kit has two of the engine mounts cut out, and trimmed to fit under these SRB skirts. Two F-1 engines are then assembled, the smaller feed pipes trimmed so they fit inside the inverted SRB skirts' fairings, and once painted, glued in place.

Attaching the Boosters to the External Tank

The final construction of these new 'LRB' fly-back boosters is how they attach to the External Tank. Because they are wider than the SRBs, and taking the wings into account, a lot wider, they can't be attached in the standard SRB positions – that is, at right angles to the Orbiter, as the wings would touch. Consequently, either they have to be angled so the wings don't touch, or they must not be positioned directly opposite each other, but angled around the ET. For this build they were offered up to the External Tank, and juggled so the wings nearer to the Orbiter obviously didn't touch the Orbiter, but also that the opposite wings of the LRB did not touch each other.

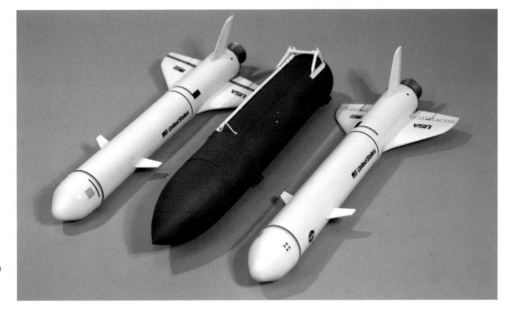

Lining up the new liquid fuel/fly-back booster with a conventional External Tank.

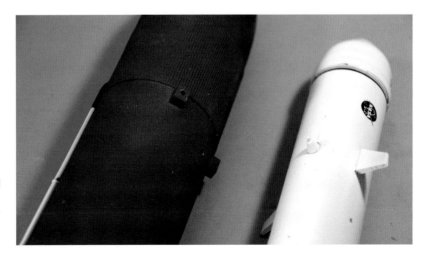

After trying various positions around the ET, locating blocks for the forward ends are glued in place. A corresponding conical pin – just visible on the white surface of the LRB – is opposite.

The two new boosters are cemented in place on the ET – note they are much further round than the original SRBs.

Another view of one of the new LRBs attached to the External Tank, which particularly shows the attachment points. The decals mainly come from Shuttle kits.

The completed Shuttle full stack, using the new fly-back Liquid-Fuelled Rocket Boosters.

Once a position was decided, it was marked in pencil and small blocks glued in place on the tank where the booster would attach. The new LRBs themselves were then marked, and a hole drilled that corresponded to the block. Small conical parts were then glued into place on the LRBs, and then glued to the blocks. Before the cement dried, the assembly was stood upright on the engine bells to ensure everything was lined up and 'square'. To this end the engine bells were cemented to a base (the usual Airfix Saturn base), as this assembly will not stand vertical without other support.

Once all this is dry, an Orbiter can be attached in the usual position. This ends up with the new LRBs further round than the 180 degrees the SRBs are in the standard set-up, but in many ways this makes more dynamic sense. But anyway, with the Shuttles as they flew, the SSMEs on the Orbiter were way off centre to the SRB engines – but the full-stack configuration still flew.

CHAPTER 10

SHUTTLE-C FOR CARGO

By the early 1970s the cost of getting payloads into orbit was being seen as a restriction on what could be done within the space programme at large. The use of these technologies significantly to bring down the cost of getting big loads into space attracted scientists and engineers to their wider use. Over time, two categories emerged: the Shuttle-C concept for replacing the winged Orbiter with a cargo pod, sending unmanned payloads into orbit, and the Shuttle-Derived Vehicle (SDV). The SDV would use Shuttle elements in a completely different way, to come up with a heavy-lifter replacing the Saturn IB and the Saturn V of a former generation.

The origin of Shuttle-C began with studies during the first half of the 1970s and immediately after the commitment to build a reusable system. There was considerable enthusiasm for building a heavy-lift capability for the mid-term future prospects of the space programme. By taking out support systems for a human presence in the Orbiter and by removing the wings and tail, the Shuttle could be adapted into a heavy-lifter by juggling the various elements and significantly increasing the payload capacity.

The first formal study began in July 1975 with a contract to the Boeing Company for a detailed design and recovery analysis for the lower elements, and a subcontract to Grumman Aerospace for upper stages and payloads analysis. The definition of terms was wide, embracing payload options from 132,300lb (60,000kg) to 992,250lb (450,000kg). The payload spread was divided into five separate classes, Classes 1 and 2 representing payload bands between the lowest to 298,000lb (135,173kg). These formed the core for Shuttle-C proposals.

Classes 1 and 2 produced four candidates including a standard Solid Rocket Booster (SRB)/External Tank (ET) configuration, another with two SRBs each side of the ET, a third with a new liquid propellant booster with the ET on top, and a fourth with a more powerful fly-back booster. All four adopted a recoverable propulsion capsule essentially duplicating the three SSMEs (Space Shuttle Main Engines) and the two orbital manoeuvring pods of the standard Orbiter and a solid propellant retro-pack for de-orbit.

Led by the Marshall Space Flight Center, new concepts included the SRB-X, a 'single-stick' SRB supporting an upper stage that could be supplemented for lift-off by two strap-on SRBs for added capability. The 'side-mount' cargo vehicle would be the Shuttle-C concept with a canister 90ft (27.4m) long and 25ft (7.62m) in diameter, and a Class 1 payload capacity of 132,300lb (60,000kg). With equal lift capacity, an 'in-line' cargo launcher would place Shuttle engines beneath a cryogenic stage topped with suitable upper stage and flanked by SRBs.

A hybrid concept would combine the LRB (Liquid Rocket Booster) Shuttle with the 'side-mount' cargo canister for carrying about 165,000lb (74,844kg) into orbit. Of diminishing return, the 'aft cargo carrier' concept would attach a large payload canister with about twice the volume of the Orbiter payload bay and, with a diameter of 27ft (8.22m), provide space for large payloads.

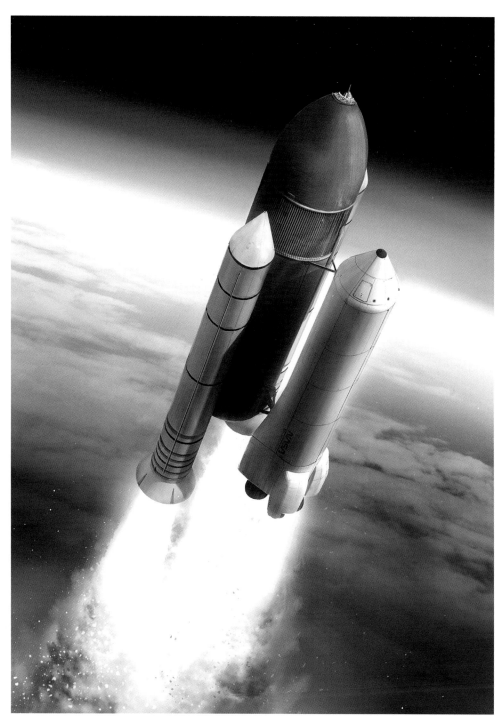

With the Orbiter replaced by a cargo pod and the aft end of the Orbiter duplicating the propulsion section, a Shuttle-C ascends into orbit.

HLV Configuration

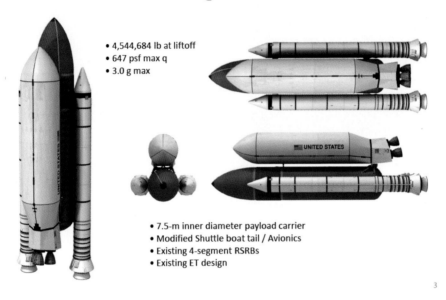

- 4,544,684 lb at liftoff
- 647 psf max q
- 3.0 g max

- 7.5-m inner diameter payload carrier
- Modified Shuttle boat tail / Avionics
- Existing 4-segment RSRBs
- Existing ET design

UNITED STATES

The general layout of the unmanned Shuttle-C configuration as it might have been developed.

3

Block I & Block II HLV Carrier Design Payload Envelopes

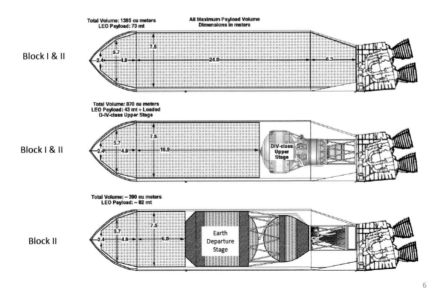

Block I & II

Total Volume: 1385 cu meters
LEO Payload: 73 mt
All Maximum Payload Volume
Dimensions in meters
7.5
5.7
2.4
4.9
24.6
6.3

Block I & II

Total Volume: 870 cu meters
LEO Payload: 43 mt + Loaded
D-IV-class Upper Stage
7.5
5.7
2.4
4.9
16.9
DIV-class Upper Stage

Block II

Total Volume: ~ 390 cu meters
LEO Payload: ~ 62 mt
7.5
5.7
2.4
4.9
6.0
Earth Departure Stage

Various Shuttle-C layouts showing an all-cargo version (top) with upper stages for sending payloads to deep-space destinations.

6

Many conceptual designs for what was now referred to as the 'propulsion module' (PM) carrying the three SSMEs were presented. The Martin Marietta PM would have been a half-cone in shape with the blunt aft end carrying the engines and the pointed forward section shaped for re-entry. It had a length of 39.4ft (12m), a maximum diameter of 26ft (7.9m), an empty weight of 67,000lb (30,391kg) and 66,968lb (30,376kg) for launch including 20,976lb (9,514kg) for the three SSMEs.

Known as the Shuttle-C cargo element (SCE), the payload pod could have been sized according to the mass and volumetric requirements of the customer. These could have been NASA, the Department of Defense, commercial companies or research organisations. The payload range was between 82,750lb (37,535kg) and 156,000lb (70,760kg).

On 20 July 1989 President George H.W. Bush made a major speech at the National Air and Space Museum in Washington, DC, in which he put his administration behind the Space Exploration Initiative (SEI). Only five years after his predecessor had launched the space station programme, Bush tasked Americans to return to the Moon and send humans to Mars. But like previous attempts to revitalise a post-Apollo programme of deep-space exploration, it died on the vine. And when the Shuttle-C User Conference heard about highly cost-effective means of gaining access to space, it fell on largely deaf ears.

Conference attendees began their last day touring the Shuttle-C Engineering Development Unit at the Marshall Center, and had the opportunity to look round the space station mock-up before convening for a final summary. All 350 attendees agreed that Shuttle-C would be better placed within the pantheon of expendable launch vehicles, rather than framed as a centrepiece for a new space programme; after all, it was a truck, and not a radical new means of putting humans into space.

If anything at all had been learned since men first landed on the Moon it was that the people factor, not trucks, that collected dollars in Congress. The Shuttle-C concept was, once again, shelved. But while down, it was not out and would be brought back again for another dusting off.

The two most commonly available Space Shuttle kits in 1:144 scale: the Revell and the Airfix. Here, both are in full-stack configuration, so include the booster section. (Revell also makes the Orbiter by itself.)

MODELLING THE CARGO SHUTTLE

The Space Shuttle system was eventually defined as being a crewed Orbiter spacecraft, powered by three SSMEs that were fed by liquid fuels during launch from the giant External Tank (ET). The whole ensemble was boosted by two massive SRBs – Solid-Fuel Rocket Boosters – fitted either side of the ET. The Orbiter and SRBs were recoverable, but not the ET.

Airfix versus Revell

As most Shuttle components are involved with this build, this is also an ideal time to examine the way the main two Space Shuttle kits – those from Airfix and Revell – go together, in particular concerning the way the SRBs attach to the External Tank, but also the way the Orbiter attaches to the tank.

The SRB attachment points to the External Tank are obviously fine in 1:1 (full size), but are very fragile in 1:144 scale – the scale of the widely available Shuttle full stack kits from Airfix and Revell. In reality the SRBs are attached to the ET at two points, one at the top, near the corrugated section of the External

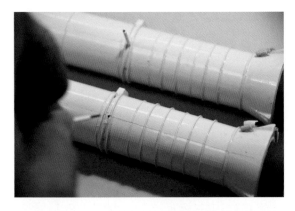

Applicable to any full-stack Shuttle build, the lower ends of the SRBs can be strengthened by drilling a small hole in both the SRB and a corresponding hole in the tank, into which a short length of metal rod can be superglued.

Similarly the top mounting point of the Orbiter – or equivalent – can be strengthened. Here is the Airfix kit, though the Revell Orbiter is much the same. Left: the stock kit using the supplied plastic part. Centre: a short metal rod superglued into the ET, with the stock plastic cut and attached either side. Right: a new, all-metal attachment point made and glued to the same holes.

Tank, and the second at the bottom: here there are three thin struts on each side, which, by the very nature of getting them down to 1:144 scale, become extremely thin and fragile.

Of the two companies, the Revell method of attaching SRBs to the ET works somewhat better than the Airfix method. The Airfix kit has a small – non-scale – pin halfway along the SRBs that fits a corresponding hole in the ET. And that, and the small struts below, is it. The Revell kit also has the lower struts, but the top of the SRB has an angled peg and corresponding slot in the ET, which is far stronger. The Revell kit also supplies a base that has a semblance to the actual Shuttle launch pad, as carried by the CT (crawler transporter) from VAB (Vehicle Assembly Building) at the Cape, to the launch pad.

Consequently, the finished full-stack Shuttle is displayed in a vertical stance. The base also has large location 'pegs' over which the SRBs slide, and if they are glued in place, the ET and Orbiter will be held securely.

However, the Airfix kit uses an adapted base originally intended for its large 1:24-scale aircraft kits, holding them in the 'flying pose'. Here, this does admittedly show the Shuttle also in a 'flying pose' (albeit one at really too shallow an angle), with the attachment point holes to the stand adaptor built into the External Tank. To display any Shuttle build based on the Airfix kit, this method does work – but the assembly has to be very thoroughly cemented together and then frankly never moved!

But things can be strengthened with both kits.

The top attachment of the SRBs is probably adequate in the Revell kit, but for the Airfix, simply drill a small hole through the moulded-in attachment point at the very top of the SRB, and a corresponding hole in the ET, and superglue in a short length of metal rod. The non-scale pin in the centre can then simply be removed.

Both manufacturers' kits also benefit from this method at the lower end of the SRBs. Retain the scale struts, but drill a similar hole to the top, at the very centre of the SRB, between these struts, and again a corresponding hole in the ET, and join with a length of metal rod. This is non-prototypical, but is unlikely to be noticed, and will greatly assist in retaining the build's integrity.

There is a similar situation with attaching the Shuttle Orbiter – or for that matter any similar craft – to the boosters. The aft end of the Orbiter has two locating holes, where pins on the support cradle fit. However, the forward end of the Orbiter is attached under its nose by – as with the SRB connectors – a very thin 'A'-shaped (or inverted 'V' if you prefer) moulding with an even thinner pin. If the Orbiter – or any other payload – is firmly cemented at the aft end to take the main weight, and the pin fitted to the forward end and the model never moved, it will – probably – survive. But any movement at all will threaten its stability, especially if you want to have a booster section that can be fitted with various loads, so the 'payload' is continuously being moved and replaced – so there has to be another way.

Consequently, for strength, this 'A'- (or 'V'-) shaped part can be replaced with either a non-proto-typical rod straight into the centre of the External Tank – cut the plastic part in half and superglue its

leg to the new pin – or make a whole new 'A'-shaped part from thin metal rod, bent to shape.

To display the Airfix kit especially, the stands supplied with the Airfix Saturn IB and Saturn V kits can be used, or any suitably sized piece of wood, appropriately finished.

Orbiting Cargo

With all these components in development, ideas were soon being put forward as to how the new hardware could be put to other purposes. Using the booster section, the External Tank and the SRBs, as planned, some ideas used this ensemble to lift payloads other than the crewed Orbiter. Admittedly the Orbiter itself was designed to carry cargo – hence being built around the cargo bay. But its size was limited – 60ft (18.3m) long by 15ft (4.6m) wide – and so payloads had to be built around what could be fitted. The Hubble Space Telescope, launched by Shuttle Mission STS-31 in 1990, ended up the size it did because it was built to the maximum size that would fit Discovery's cargo bay.

Consequently, one proposal was that the Shuttle C would utilise the new hardware built for the crewed Shuttle missions, but would – in theory – allow for greater weights to be launched, and would promise a faster turnaround, as the environmental requirements for a human crew did not have to be taken into consideration.

These ideas were started around 1984 and lasted for a decade, and fell roughly into two types. One arm of these proposals would replace the Orbiter with a similar craft, probably based on existing Orbiter hardware, but would involve one-off missions only to carry cargo, and the craft would not be destined to return to Earth. These tended to use the shape and size of the crewed Orbiter's cargo bay, so were limited to that size, but in theory would be able to carry a heavier payload than the standard crewed Orbiter's 65,000lb (29,000kg) (around 30 tons). The existing SRBs and ET would be used, and the new 'C' version of the Orbiter would be fitted with the Aerojet Rocketdyne RS-25 rocket engine, otherwise

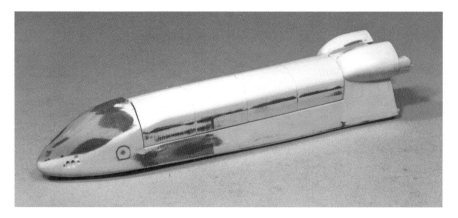

An Airfix Shuttle Orbiter, with the wings removed and the cockpit area filled in with plastic sheet and model putty. Sanded smooth, but not yet painted.

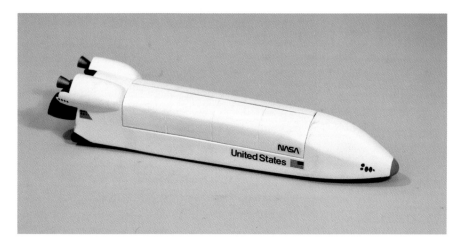

A version of the Shuttle-C that uses the shape of the Orbiter, without wings. The original forward section has been fared over to create a streamlined shape without the cockpit windows.

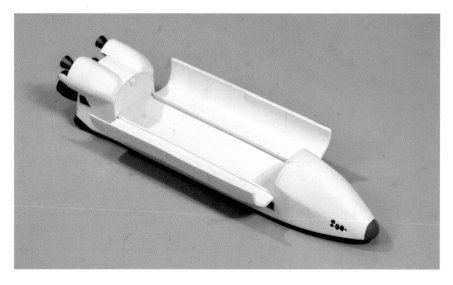

The 'Orbiter-shaped' Shuttle C, with the doors open. This is a modified Airfix kit that does not have operating doors, but here is made to work with a length of plastic rod. In addition an empty cargo bay has been made from sheet styrene.

The Orbiter-based Shuttle-C, attached to the standard booster section.

known as SSMEs, still fed by the fuel in the External Tank.

A More Advanced Proposal

A more advanced proposal would still use the SRBs and ET, but there would be a completely new – and larger – payload section, though carried in the same position as the Orbiter, and still powered by the same SSMEs.

Building variations of the Shuttle-C concept starts with one of the Space Shuttle kits, and depending on what is being built, a few other parts could be necessary.

The most straightforward adaptation is to use an existing Shuttle Orbiter, either unbuilt, or maybe recycle an existing kit. Only the fuselage section is needed, so if using the Airfix kit the lower wing section is one piece, so the central section of the fuselage needs separating from the lower wings, and cementing to the two fuselage halves. The Revell Orbiter has the wings – top and bottom halves – separate, so it is purely a case of omitting them, though in both cases, the subsequent gaps will need filling. The tail and rudder are also not needed, so, as both Airfix and Revell (and all the others) have this attached to the main body, they need sawing off, and any gaps filled.

The crewed nose section also needs 'filling in' as there are no cockpit windows, but some streamlining – for launch – is required. Here the area in front of the windows needs filling in, though the exact shape and cross-section is not important. Here it was first roughly filled in with scrap plastic, and then car-body filler applied. This type of two-part resin can be applied in thick quantities as it cures chemically – it does not 'dry' by evaporation, as does standard modelling filler or putty, which consequently needs to be applied in thinner layers. Final finishes can be made with putty, and when all is dry/cured, can be wet-and-dry sanded to a smooth finish. One point to note: be sure to retain the RCS (Reaction Control System) nozzles on the sides of the nose at the very least, as they would be required once in orbit.

The aft end of the 'C' body still needs the plate for the SSME bells, though there could be the option of using only two engines, omitting the upper one. However, the OMS (Orbital Manoeuvring System) pods need to be fitted, because once the craft is separated from the External Tank, the SSMEs lack their fuel, so manoeuvring in orbit uses the OMS engines. This aft section also has its own RCS nozzles, which can be picked out with paint.

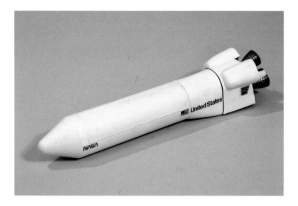

A version of the Shuttle-C that only uses the Orbiter engine pod. This is now attached to a new forward section based on a 1½in tube with a new conical top.

Building the Cargo Bay

Both Airfix and Revell's Orbiters have separate cargo-bay doors, though the Revell kit has the advantage of not only hinged doors, but a cargo-bay interior that is separately moulded from any payload. The Airfix, on the other hand, not only lacks hinged doors (though they are arguably slightly better moulded), but the interior has a Spacelab set-up moulded in: this may have been easier from Airfix's point of view, but it means that if any other payload is wanted, a new interior will have to be built. This is actually not that difficult, as it can be formed from lengths of plastic sheet. The Airfix doors can also be made to 'operate' by cementing thin plastic rod to the inner edges, and drilling holes in the fore and aft bulkheads. Extra detailing – and the addition of any payload – is then up to the builder.

An alternative approach is to use only the rear engine section from one of the Shuttle kits, and to make a new forward section from round tube. A 1½in (38mm) tube will match the top of the engine section circumference of the Orbiter, though the underside will need filling to blend it from the flat surface of the engines to the round cross-section of the new 'fuselage'. Again, car-filler resin will be ideal. Also a nose cone will have to be sourced: the ubiquitous

This alternative Shuttle-C is attached to the standard booster section.

top section of the Skylab Saturn V from Airfix is one option, while the outline of payload doors can be added with thin plastic strips. The engine set-up could vary. Here the standard three SSMEs were used, and although the OMS nozzles were not, their pods remained.

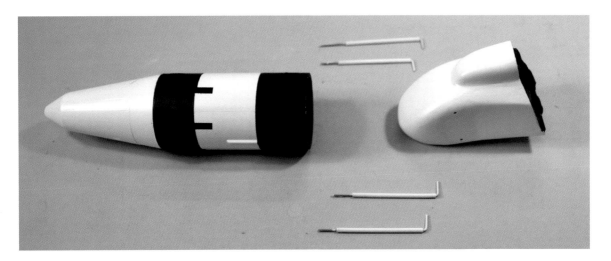

Rebuilding an existing conversion where the Shuttle Orbiter engine pod has been removed from an Orbiter, and a new forward end created from a wood block, carved to shape. The payload is a modified S-IVB stage from the Saturn IB or V kit, with a new nose cone made from the SLA and the BPC glued at the apex. Four metal rods with plastic covering are cut and bent to connect the engine pod to this new upper stage.

Building a Recoverable Pod

A third proposal used the rear section of the Orbiter, with SSMEs and OMS, but in a separate 'pod' that could be recoverable. This was attached, via open supports, to a forward section that would end up in orbit. For this, the whole end section of the Shuttle Orbiter was assembled, but the OMS pods were moved to be positioned 'top and bottom' of the main SSME set-up. This assembly was then sawn away from the main Orbiter body. A new front 'streamlined section' (that would contain the parachutes for recovery) was created from hard balsa wood, carved to shape (the actual shape isn't vital), sanded, sealed and primed. The front face of the engine section was then filled with plastic sheet, and the two parts superglued together.

The payload section was built from a Saturn S-IVB stage (available in both Saturn V and Saturn IB kits, being the third stage of the first, and the second stage of the second). The S-IVB stage, with its single J-2 rocket engine, can be built as per the instructions, while the nose cone was built from the SLA (Spacecraft Lunar Adaptor, which housed the Lunar Module) that

sits on the top of the SVI-B anyway. The opening at the top, where the Apollo Service Module would fit, is instead covered with the conical BPC (Boost Protection Cover) that would fit over the Command Module. This has the four holes for the launch escape system rocket legs, but these are cut or sawn off, and the holes filled if necessary, and glued direct to the SLA section.

Four holes were then drilled into the sides of the 'engine pod', and four holes into the end of the S-VIB stage, each approximately 1mm in diameter. This is to allow the two sections to be linked by four connecting rods. These were constructed from a 2in (50mm) length of EMA pipe (P(-)3), approximately 2.5mm in diameter, with a 1mm brass rod slid down inside, increasing the total length of reach to 2½in (64mm) plus another ¼in (6mm) each end. One end is bent 90 degrees to fit the holes in the engine pod, while the other ends are slid into the drilled holes in the lower part of the S-IVB stage. All ends are then superglued in place.

The second idea was to abandon any Orbiter design and purely use the engine pod – much as the previous conversion – but to attach it to a much larger payload stage. This new stage could have

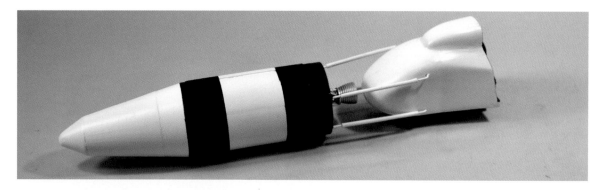

The completed two stages of a cargo Shuttle – payload and engine pod, connected together by the new struts.

This new uncrewed payload stage attached to the standard Shuttle booster section.

been large – in fact it could have been the size of the whole External Tank, so in fact one option would be to use the parts of a second External Tank. However, one slight problem here is that the ET has almost too much detailing, and specialist detailing as an External Tank at that. The Revell version also has the corrugated section round the upper end moulded in, which, it could be argued, is not suitable for what is meant to be a different stage. The Airfix one doesn't have these corrugations moulded in, it uses decals – but even here the pipe details, and in fact the whole look of this structure, does make it somewhat stand out as 'the External Tank'.

So it might be better to go for a whole new piece of tubing. The External Tank is 2¼in (64mm) in diameter, and EMA tube is available in that size. However, the exact diameter is perhaps not that important, so, lacking any EMA tube, other tube of other diameters could be used.

This new structure of course needs a nose cone, though – and assuming any new tube is not wider than the diameter of the ET – the top could be cut off an External Tank, and that adapted. This approach was used here, but just to make it slightly different to the tank, the top end was sawn off, and a different cone shape, another EMA part, was used. It is actually the top of the 90-degree cone – part VC-90 (where it is a separate part) – and that was cemented in place. Slightly perversely, having not used an ET because it had those 'corrugations', here a strip of corrugated embossed plastic sheet was used, but glued in a

The aft ends of three Shuttle-C concepts showing three different engine set-ups. Left: one that uses all five rocket engines – three SSMEs and two OMS, but the OMS pods are moved 'top and bottom' on the pod. Centre: three SSMEs are used, but no OMS, though the pods remain. Right: the pods and two OMS engines remain, but the SSMEs are reduced to two.

Making a brand new cargo pod for a 'heavy lift' version. It is based on a section of 2¼in tubing and a new faring, made from the top of an External Tank. The nose of the latter has also been removed and in its place will be the top of an EMA cone – seen centre right.

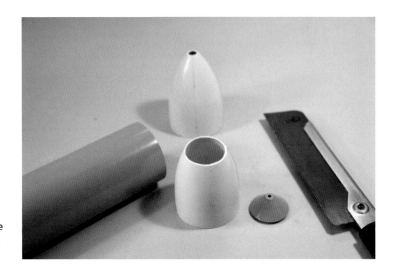

Cutting the engine pod from a Shuttle Orbiter, here the Airfix version. The tube has an end plate added, to which the engine pod can be cemented.

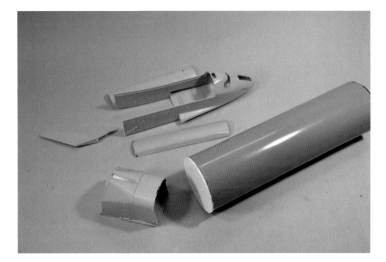

Initial filling-in of the engine pod, here using a section from a cone found in the bits and pieces box.

Starting to fill in the gaps of the engine pod to the main body tube, using car resin filler. The mixed resin cures fairly quickly (depending on how much catalyst has been added), but reaches an intermediate stage where it is 'set', but not 'hard', so can be trimmed with a sharp blade, before it is sanded. Here a Stanley-type blade is used, but not in the knife itself, as it is easier to handle – with care.

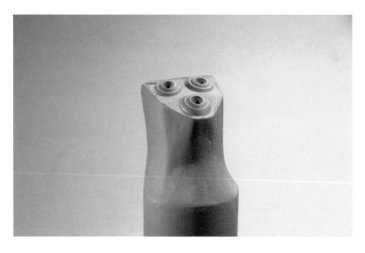

The engine pod fitted to the main body, with the base filler trimmed and sanded, and primed – which will show up what still needs to be done. The final filling can be done with model filler as the layers will only need to be very thin.

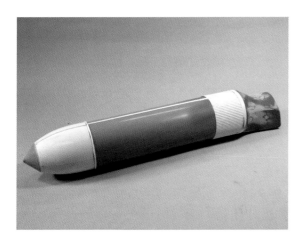

The heavy-lift payload section, assembled but not painted. Left to right the sections are as follows: the top of an EMA 90-degree cone; the cut-down top of the External Tank; the EMA 2¼in diameter tube; a corrugated section added from embossed plastic sheet; and the engine pod.

different position, around the aft end of the main cylindrical tube, similar to that found on a Saturn V.

The engine pod was built round the section cut from the Shuttle Orbiter. The two OMS pods were not fitted, nor was the beaver-tail airbrake. Most of the work then needed was to attach this pod to the end of the main stage tube, and to blend it in.

First the end of the tube was blanked off with sheet plastic, and the engine pod cemented in place, with the flat section against one edge of the tubing. The resulting gaps around this were then filled with scrap shapes (a half cone was found in the bits and pieces box, which came in useful), and glued in place. Then car filler was used to fill in around most of the gaps, and sanded; any gaps still remaining were filled again, then more sanding, and any small remaining gaps filled with model filler.

Once all was dry and sanded smooth, it was primed and all painted gloss white. The holes under the engine pod remained, to attach the lower section of the External Tank in its full-stack configuration, and a new hole drilled further up to correspond to the Orbiter's nose attachment point.

Adding the Decals

Decals are added to all these conversions, and given they are Shuttle-based, a selection from those kits will be the most appropriate starting point. Both Airfix and Revell kits have vastly increased the number of decals provided. The first issue of the Airfix kit had nine decals (and one of those was the name plate), the second version had 58, the most recent has increased this to 127! So with a recent kit especially

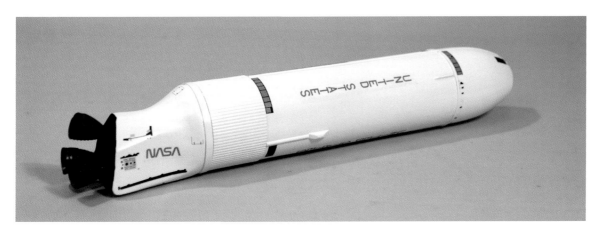

The heavy-lift payload, painted gloss white, with decals from various Shuttle and Saturn kits applied. The engine pod is finished in the standard Orbiter finish of a matt-black engine bulkhead and gunmetal engine bells.

there should be enough to choose from. But remember you are not restricted to 'just' the Shuttle kits, there are plenty of alternatives decals in kits, aircraft especially, and stock lines of many widths and block decals are available from many manufacturers.

Displaying the Models

Given that these conversions are all designed to fit the standard booster set-up of the Space Shuttle, the finished models will sit on their SRB nozzles. The Revell kits are aided as they are designed to stand on the supplied 'launch pad' base, with large locators for the SRB rocket nozzles. The Airfix version is intended to be displayed in 'flight mode' (which will mean everything has to be glued very firmly in place), but it will also sit on a flat base, on the SRB nozzles – the rectangular base supplied in the Airfix Saturn V and IB kits could be suitable. However, you will find that although the SRBs and ET by themselves will stand upright without further support, by the time a payload (Orbiter or otherwise) is hung on one side, it all gets rather unbalanced, so the SRB nozzles may very well have to be glued down.

The heavy-lift payload attached to the standard Shuttle booster section. Note that the new stage is basically the same diameter as the External Tank.

CHAPTER 11

HEAVY LIFT SHUTTLE

In 1983 Martin Marietta produced a pragmatic analysis of opportunities through scavenging technology from the Shuttle programme. Studies of the 1970s had proposed the Propulsion Module (PM) containing three Space Shuttle Main Engines (SSMEs) from the 'side-mount' configuration for Shuttle-C. It was the simplest adaptation, the core stage being the External Tank flanked by two Solid Rocket Boosters (SRBs) but with the PM on one side at the base and a payload canister on top of the External Tank.

If an upper stage was required to push the payload into orbit, the PM would return to Earth on a suborbital, ballistic trajectory after separating during the ascent. Designated 'Inline-I', this

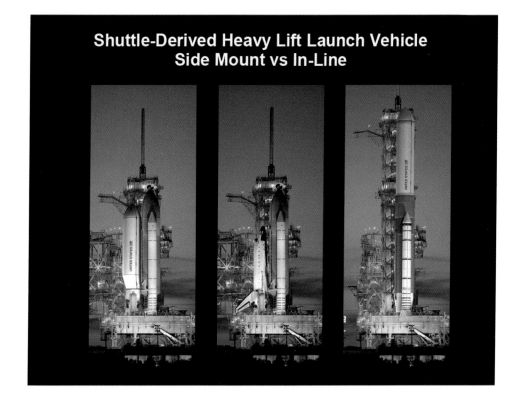

The further development of Shuttle-C resulted in separate concepts for larger vehicles based on the in-line configuration with the propulsion unit at the base of a heavy-lift launch vehicle.

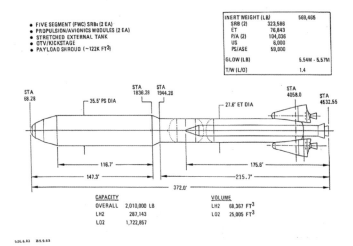

INERT WEIGHT (LB)	569,465
SRB (2)	323,586
ET	76,843
P/A (2)	104,036
US	6,000
PS/ASE	59,000
GLOW (LB)	5.54M - 5.57M
T/W (L/O)	1.4

- FIVE SEGMENT (FWC) SRBs (2 EA)
- PROPULSION/AVIONICS MODULES (2 EA)
- STRETCHED EXTERNAL TANK
- OTV/KICKSTAGE
- PAYLOAD SHROUD (~122K FT³)

CAPACITY		VOLUME	
OVERALL	2,010,000 LB	LH2	68,367 FT³
LH2	287,143	LO2	25,005 FT³
LO2	1,722,857		

The Inline-II concept had two propulsion modules and an oversize payload volume.

- FIVE SEGMENT/FILAMENT CASE (2 EA)
- PROPULSION/AVIONICS MODULE/3 SSMEs (2 EA)
- CORE TANK (33 FT X 197.8 FT)
- CENTAUR F (KICK STAGE)
- PAYLOAD SHROUD (~192K FT³)

INERT WEIGHT (LB)	662,242
SRB (2)	323,586
CT	115,006
P/A (2)	127,114
US	6,091
PS	90,445
GLOW (MLB)	6.7-6.75
T/W (L/O)	1.46

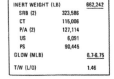

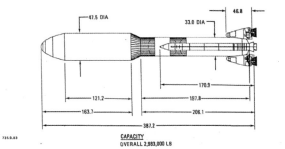

CAPACITY	
OVERALL 2,983,000 LB	

The Inline-III design with the growth payload canister and high payload capacity in the final HLLV 'stretch' of the Shuttle-C concept prior to relocating the propulsion units underneath the core stage propellant tank.

configuration used two SSMEs operating at 108 per cent thrust and could place 150,000lb (68,040kg) in orbit.

The 'Inline II' configuration had two propulsion modules at 180-degree intervals at the base of a stretched External Tank, and two longer and more powerful SRBs each having a length of 175.5ft (53.49m). An upper stage would have been desirable for maximum payload potential. The very large payload section would have had a length of 147.3ft (44.89m) and a diameter of 35.5ft (10.8m), with a total vehicle height of 372ft (113.3m).

The option of a payload canister with still greater internal volume and a diameter of 47.5ft (14.47m) was designated 'Inline III', and would have had a Centaur upper stage; the overall vehicle length was 387.2ft (118m).

It was the recoverable elements that helped show significant reductions in operating costs per unit mass of payload from the 'Inline I' to the 'Inline III' concepts. But the development time and the costs involved again showed, as it had with the Shuttle, that only through a traffic model involving high flight rates could any financial advantage be achieved.

Rockwell International was keen to base future possibilities on the Orbiter, which they had the contract to build. Martin Marietta was building the External Tank, which would always be a core structure for upgrades and growth versions. Rocketdyne, another division of Rockwell, was assembling the SSMEs, another key element for capitalising on reusability and commonality.

Under a Shuttle Growth Study contract from the Marshall Space Flight Center, Rockwell studied water-recoverable, liquid-propellant boosters for an unmanned Shuttle derivative with clamshell doors. But in these studies, the boosters were the core stage, and the SSMEs underneath the ET were replaced by more powerful cryogenic engines.

Rockwell extended its liquid-propellant booster studies to provide optional configurations for very heavy launchers, which is where the Heavy Lift Launch Vehicle (HLLV) came into its own at a particularly propitious time. With talk of extending space flight operations back to the Moon and on to Mars, by the 1990s the availability of heavy lifters was a bonus. In some of these configurations, with four liquid-propellant boosters clustered as a core stage, a payload of 360,000lb (163,296kg) could be placed in low Earth orbit.

Research into growth versions for the HLLV studies had the effect of folding back the analysis to include modifications to the Shuttle Orbiter so that it could take advantage of the increased lift capacity of the modified boosters – both solid and liquid-propellant types. With stress factors taken into account, and using liquid-propellant boosters, a 15ft (4.57m) long barrel section was added to extend the fuselage, with the payload bay increased by that amount to a total length of 75ft (22.86m).

In this form it could accommodate a payload of 100,000lb (45,360kg) but would require a new wing root and carry-through structure for increased landing loads while retaining the outer wing sections. And with the same landing loads as those accepted by the original Orbiter, the stretched vehicle could return with the same weight it carried into orbit.

The HLLV programme and the stimulus to do much more with Shuttle elements fed right back into Orbiter improvements. Without SSMEs, the Orbiter would have a length of 142.8ft (43.52m), and a special 'humpback' version could have provided additional volume for large payloads.

A five-segment engineering test booster was fired on 23 October 2003. This was followed by a full-scale five-segment SRB tested on 10 September 2009. Had the intended replacement for the then existing four-segment standard SRB been inducted into Shuttle operations, it would have increased payload by 20,000lb (9,072kg).

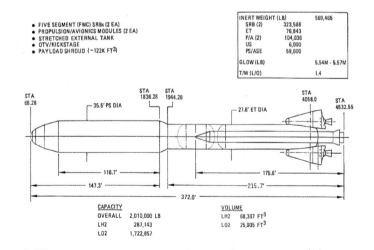

A further variation with Solid Rocket Boosters, External Tank and pods with Shuttle engines.

MODELLING THE ETs AND SRBs – OUT ON THEIR OWN

When NASA eventually decided that the Space Transportation System would consist of a crewed Orbiter, but uncrewed booster section, this meant the development of completely new systems. Besides the Orbiter, NASA ended up with a giant External Tank, the ET, and Solid-Fuelled Rocket Boosters, the SRBs. And as soon as they were in development, plans were proposed that could use the components, but in different ways.

In the end none of these came to fruition, but it is interesting to examine what could have been. These builds are also an ideal use of the 'bits and pieces' box, as many builds just use some parts in the kit, and you have 'left overs'. It is also ideal for kits that have already been built, but are now perhaps showing signs of their longevity and are about to fall apart.

The starting point for many of the builds in this chapter – the bits and pieces box (well, one of them...). This contains Space Shuttle parts and was augmented by another box that contained already built kits that had seen better days.

Shuttle Modification Using Four Boosters

One early proposal, which didn't require any new hardware, was to double the number of SRBs. Consequently the full stack – the general name for the assembled Space Shuttle on the launch pad – would be one Orbiter, one ET, and four SRBs. These would be staggered either side of the Orbiter's mounting position, one placed slightly nearer the Orbiter, the other further back.

This is an ideal starter project for Shuttle modifications as all it requires is one standard Shuttle full-stack kit, and two extra SRBs, either from a second kit, or from that ubiquitous spares box. The Orbiter can be built 'straight out of the box', as can, basically, the External Tank and SRBs – though of course, as mentioned, the SRBs are not going to fit directly in the same positions.

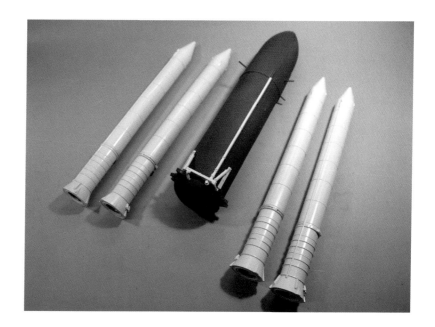

The already built four SRB section, dismantled for this rebuild. The SRBs will be resprayed with a fresh coat of gloss white paint.

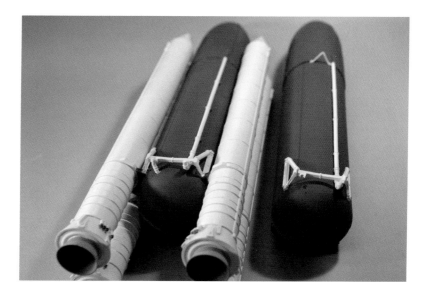

Comparing the position of the four SRBs (left) to the standard ET (right). The four SRB set-up requires the lower mounting points for the SRBs next to the Orbiter, which have the connecting legs for the Orbiter support, to be modified, and the new 'saddles' (EMA parts) to overlap these supports. (Note some of the pipe-work is omitted here for clarity.)

Attaching the Four Boosters

As the four boosters of this conversion need to be spaced round the External Tank, there is a change to their usual method of attachment. Following on to details included in Chapter 10, the top ends of each SRB were attached using the 'pin and hole' method,

but the lower ends used another approach. Using the fact that the width of the SRB around the lower attachment point is $1\frac{1}{8}$in (27.5mm) in diameter, a 'saddle' was used to attach this section to the ET, as it gives a far greater gluing area. Here, EMA parts VS-36 were used, though similar shapes could be cut from reasonably thick plastic sheet.

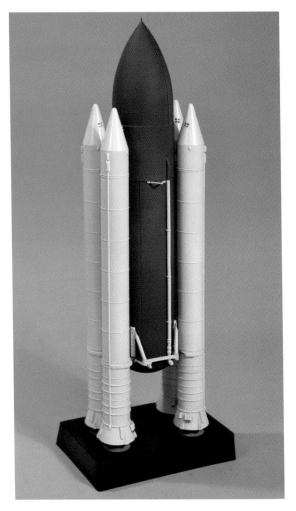

The rebuilt Shuttle booster section on a standard Airfix Saturn V base. The Orbiter is not in place, as it would obscure most of this conversion.

With the four SRBs in place, a Shuttle Orbiter can still be added, or alternatively one of the other uncrewed payloads indicated in other chapters. The completed four SRBs are also still small enough to fit an Airfix Saturn V or IB base.

Uncrewed Launches Using Three Boosters

Ideas were also proposed for uncrewed launches, some even using just the SRBs. One of these proposals used three SRBs – two in their conventional position, attached not to an ET and Orbiter, but to a third SRB, itself carrying an uncrewed payload. This is a simple conversion as it primarily uses three SRBs, and some upper stage for the central booster. It isn't quite as simple as purely attaching the two 'booster' SRBs to the central one, as the standard SRBs have a skirt section at the base. This can't really be fitted to the central SRB, as the outer SRBs will have to be bulked out where they attached to fit. Instead the skirt section is removed, so the central SRB is straight up and down. The SRB nosecone is also removed at this time, though it is reattached later.

The removal of the skirt also affects the engine plate of this central SRB, which can't be used. The standard rocket nozzle for the SRBs could be used, but without the engine plate it will disappear up inside the main tube, unless it is bulked out with thin strips of plastic, or a new, much smaller engine plate made. Alternatively – as here – another EMA part was used. These are actually 'reducers' for joining one size pipe to another, but to this end, this means they are cones, and make good rocket nozzles. (Used here was a R(W)324 that reduces $1^{1}/_{8}$in [27.5mm] down to ¾in [19mm]. Note the 'R' is for 'reducer'; the 'W' in brackets is the colour of the plastic, here white. Other colours, and hence other letter codes, have been available.)

Even with the central skirt removed, the outer SRBs need to be moved slightly out from the central one, primarily to leave room for the central engine bell. Here small EMA parts were used, but frankly any suitably sized pieces of plastic will suffice,

Slots were cut in the ET, the ones closest to the Orbiter part using the existing slot moulded in for the Orbiter support. This means the strut base and this Orbiter support have to be trimmed to fit. A matching slot was cut further round, so the two SRBs each side sit equidistant to the original centre line for the single SRB. The ideal gap between the main bodies of each SRB pair is ½in (12.5mm). This just allows the lower skirt section at the base of each SRB to have a gap – it is admittedly only about $^{1}/_{16}$in (1mm), but it is a gap.

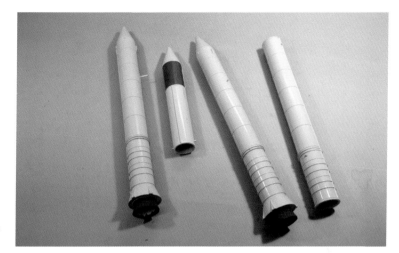

Bits for the 'Three SRBs' conversion collected together. In the end not all these parts were used, and some were replaced with new SRB parts.

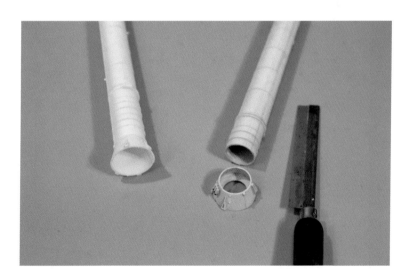

The 'skirt' end of the central SRB has to be cut away, otherwise the outer SRBs would have to sit further away from the centre.

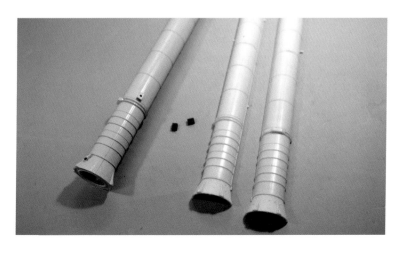

For the 'Three SRB' build, the outer SRBs need to be positioned away from the central SRB. Here, small square mounting blocks were used. These were actually EMA parts, but any polystyrene strip cut down to size will suffice.

The completed 'Three SRB' launcher. The original upper stage (from its original build) was reused, and repainted. This consists of a similar diameter tube (to an SRB), with the original SRB nose cone on top. Decals, some from the Airfix Saturn IB, have also been applied.

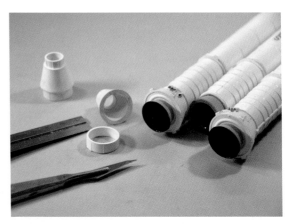

Even with the outer SRBs slightly away from the central, this still means the existing engine bell will not fit the central SRB, so a 'reducer' (an EMA part) was adapted. It is seen intact on the upper left, and then with the large connector section cut off, below. This then drops into the modified central SRB, and is painted to match the other engine bells.

(if EMA parts are used they are already drilled with holes).

This creates the launch rocket, and attached to the top of the central stage can be anything you want. Here a short length of plastic tube of a similar diameter to the SRB – 1in (25mm) – was glued on top of the SRB, and the SRB nose cone added on top of that. Alternatively a stage, such as the top stage of an Ariane 4 kit (from Heller), could be adapted, which gives a wider payload diameter for added interest.

The SRBs – all three – can be finished in the same way as they would be to launch the Shuttle Orbiter, so you can add black stripes, red stripes or yellow stripes to your own liking.

A Short External Tank

One uncrewed launcher that uses Shuttle booster components involved a shortened External Tank; the SRBs are short by one segment, and a payload upper

and will be far cheaper. Similar to the methods described in Chapter 10, drill through the central SRB; thread through a piece of plastic or metal rod, and drill similar holes for attachment to the block

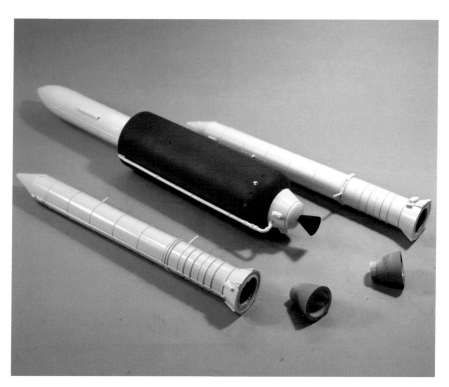

Components for the conversion for the upper payload stage to be on top of the External Tank. The tank is shortened, basically by removing the corrugated section, and a new top made from part of an EMA cone. Alternatively the original top of the ET could be used, with a suitable hole cut for the new upper stage. This stage is a 1in (25mm) diameter tube, with a new conical top. One Space Shuttle Main Engine is used at the base, with the fuel pipe-work of the ET modified to fit their new positions.

stage is built into the top of the ET. In this case the Airfix kit is easier to deal with as the External Tank is in three parts – the main body, the section with the corrugations (supplied as decals in the Airfix kit) and the tapered top section. For this conversion you just need the main section up to the 'corrugations'. (If using the Revell kit, the tank needs to be cut through.)

The top of the 'short' tank was fitted with a section of a 90-degree cone taken from an EMA part (VC-90). These cones have indentations inside, showing where they can be cut down. Here the inner section was cut to 1¼in (30mm), so a piece of EMA tube of the same diameter (VT-125) was slid down and cemented in place. However, as this again is purely speculative, any similar diameter tube could be used, and the joining section does not even need to be a cone. The top section of the actual tank could be used – join it on without the 'corrugated' section – and cut a suitable diameter hole. Even the

base section of the tank from another kit could be adapted.

However made, the top of the new upper stage needs a conical top. The one here was turned from hard balsa wood, sanded, then suitably sealed and painted, though sources of cones are also found throughout the other chapters for other builds.

The SRBs are shortened by one segment, otherwise they sit too high against the External Tank. If using the Airfix kit, the non-scale attachment pin halfway along the SRB is still there, so the SRBs could be attached in the standard way. However, the methods described in Chapter 10 will be stronger.

One point about this conversion is that there is no Orbiter, so the question could be 'What are the cryogenic fuels in the External Tank feeding?' Well, in this case it is a single SSME, placed directly under the ET, the attachment components using parts from the Airfix Apollo Saturn V.

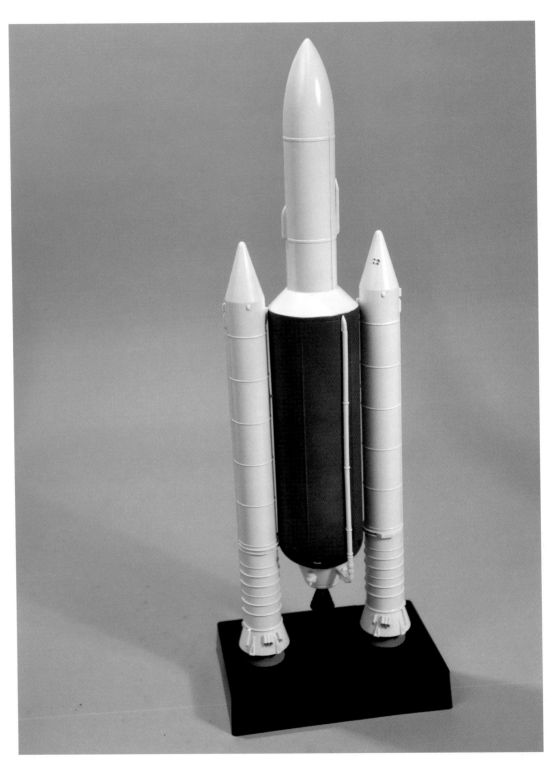

The External Tank launcher with the SRBs fitted, on a Saturn base.

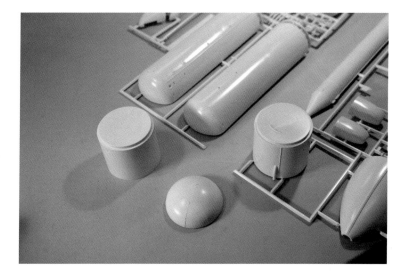

The 'underneath' payload container uses parts from a second Airfix Shuttle kit – the separated 'corrugated section'. The Revell kit will have to have this section cut from the whole tank. The base of the ET of either kit will then need cutting from the main tank.

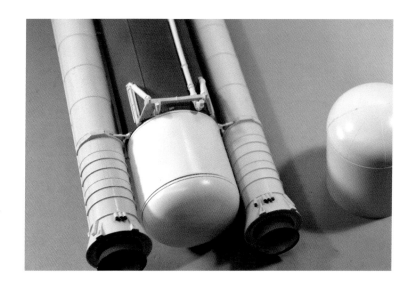

The cut base of the ET is fitted to the 'corrugated' section; then the whole assembly is turned upside down and cemented to the bottom of the External Tank.

Placing the Payload Fairing Underneath the External Tank

Another intriguing adaptation to lifting payload using the whole Shuttle full stack was to place the payload fairing not on top of the External Tank, or the side, but underneath. This is also a straightforward conversion as it uses a second External Tank 'corrugated' section – conveniently separate in the Airfix kit, though it would have to be cut from the Revell (that moulds the whole ET in two halves), and the hemispherical base cut from the ET (this will have to occur with either make). Then turn the upper section upside down, reattach the hemispherical base of the tank to this, and cement this structure to the base of the ET. It almost certainly would not have the 'brown' finish of the ET (it doesn't hold cryogenic fuels, so would not require insulation), so paint the components separately before cementing them together.

167

None of these suggestions ever saw themselves positioned on the launch pad. However, the idea of reusing these Shuttle booster components, both SRBs and External Tank, even the SSMEs, did eventually happen and formed a major part of the structures for Project Artemis.

The External Tank payload version can then have an Obiter put in place, though it is omitted here for clarity.

CHAPTER 12

THE LOST CONSTELLATIONS

The flight hardware for the project named 'Constellation' included the Solid Rocket Boosters (SRBs), the External Tank (ET) and the Space Shuttle Main Engines (SSMEs), together with a new crew-carrying spacecraft called Orion and a lunar lander called Altair for carrying astronauts down to the Moon's surface.

Ares I would lift the Orion crew capsule into Earth orbit, where it would dock with the International Space Station (ISS) or with the Earth Departure Stage (EDS) of the Ares V heavy-lift launcher. Common to both was a Rocketdyne J-2 engine. It had been developed further into the J-2X and had a thrust of 294,000lb (1,307.7kN) in its primary mode on Ares I and 242,000lb (1,076.4kN) at a variable mixture ratio for the EDS on Ares V.

In the *Constellation* mission the crew would launch in Orion on Ares I and rendezvous with the Altair and EDS placed in Earth orbit by Ares V. Orion would dock to Altair and, while the assembly was still attached to the EDS, use its J-2X engine for translunar injection. The EDS would separate leaving Orion and Altair on a three-day flight to the Moon.

On arriving in lunar orbit all crew members would move into Altair and go down to the surface, leaving Orion unattended until they returned. Altair would support up to seven surface excursions for scientific activity, with a surface stay time of up to eight days. At the end of the mission the crew would lift off using the Altair ascent stage and dock with Orion, which would return the crew to Earth and a splashdown recovery.

The two-stage launcher had a total height of 308ft (93.8m) with a maximum diameter of 18ft (5.5m) and a payload capacity of 56,000lb (25,400kg) to low Earth orbit. The Ares I booster had a length of 173ft (52.7m), a diameter of 12ft (3.65m), a mass of 1.6 million lb (726,667kg) and a nominal thrust of 3.5 million lb (15,568kN).

The first stage would burn for 2min 6sec and separate from the upper stage and Orion at an altitude of approximately 36 miles (57.9km). The J-2X would fire one second later and burn for 7min 45sec to achieve an altitude of 80.5 miles (129.5km), when Orion would separate and fire its service engine to nudge into a low Earth orbit heading for the ISS or for the Ares V EDS.

During the fall back through the atmosphere, the protective aeroshell on the booster would be jettisoned at 15,000ft (4,572m), deploying a pilot parachute of 11.5ft (3.5m), automatically extracting the 68ft (20.7m) drogue parachute to stabilise the descending capsule in the vertical. Three 68ft (45.7m) diameter main parachutes would lower the spent booster to the water for recovery.

To test the rocket a flight was scheduled for a ballistic trajectory with live first stage and dummy upper stages, spacecraft and its launch escape system. Designated the Ares I-X test, it launched from LC-39B on 28 October 2009: it caused significant pad damage, and one of the main parachutes failed, and incurred serious damage on impact with the Atlantic Ocean. A follow-up flight (Ares I-Y) was to have taken place in 2015, but was cancelled.

Hardware for the Constellation programme was a straight legacy from the Shuttle-era technology, including Ares I, which was essentially the SRB-X capable of launching an Orion-manned spacecraft.

The specification for Ares V was a trade-off between available technology, development cost, operational reliability and payload requirements. NASA accepted a configuration capable of sending 414,000lb (187,790kg) to a low Earth orbit or 133,600lb (60,600kg) to the Moon. To achieve that the vehicle had to be flexible, with options on the precise configuration. The biggest driver in the payload requirement was the Altair lander, with a weight of up to 118,188lb (53,600kg), more than three times the mass of Apollo's Lunar Module.

After trade-offs, the preferred configuration in 2008 was for a cryogenic core stage with a length of 214.8ft (65.48m) and a diameter of 32.8ft (10m). It would have supported five or six RS-68B engines at the base, each with a thrust of 660,000lb

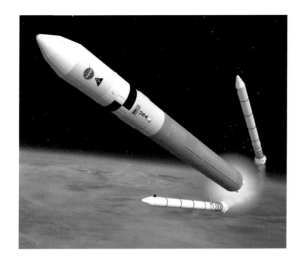

Ares V was the super-heavy lifter designed to send humans back to the Moon and eventually on to Mars.

(2,935.7kN), developed as a simplified but much more powerful version of the SSME. The core stage would be flanked by two five-segment SRBs, at 178.6ft (54.11m) somewhat longer than Shuttle SRBs. The upper stage with its single J-2X would have had a length of 75ft (22.86m), topped by a 71.1ft (21.68m) tall payload shroud.

The entire configuration would have had a total height of 360.9ft (110.01m); some variants with seven-segment solid propellant boosters could have had a height of 381.1ft (116.2m) and weighed up to 8.2 million lb (3.7 million kg). The larger solid propellant boosters would have had a length of 192.6ft (58.7m). With five RS-68B engines on dice, lift-off thrust would have been 10.1 million lb (44,924.8kN).

Launch would be preceded with ignition of the five RS-68B engines followed by the boosters, which would fire for 2min 6.6sec before separating and returning with the same recovery equipment as that for the Ares I. Core stage cut-off would occur at 5min 25.3sec at 75.75 miles (121.9km), followed immediately by ignition of the EDS stage, which would continue to fire until 12min 47sec to inject into orbit a total mass of 359,287lb (162,972kg), including the EDS and its remaining propellant and payload.

Without informing NASA personnel of its decision, on 1 February 2010 the White House summarily cancelled *Constellation* in its press conference for the next budget year, eliminating all but cancellation costs.

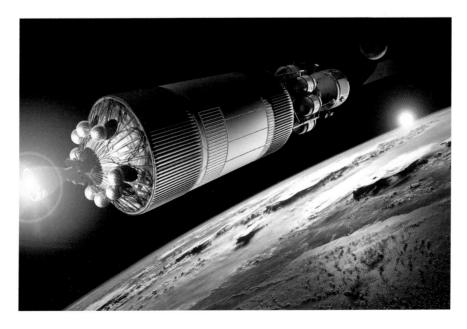

The Ares V Earth Departure Stage sends the docked Orion and Altair spacecraft off to the Moon.

MODELLING PROJECT CONSTELLATION

With the Space Shuttle reaching the end of its life, NASA had to look to another method of putting crews into space, and back to the Moon. This eventually emerged as Project Artemis – but first came Project Constellation.

One commonality with both projects was the use of tested Shuttle components, especially the Solid Rocket Boosters (SRBs) and the External Tank (ET). To this would be added a new form of 'Apollo command module' that would carry more crew, but would return Apollo-fashion with a splashdown in the ocean.

Because it was based on Shuttle hardware, it is quite straightforward to recreate the Project Constellation rockets, using existing Space Shuttle kits plus some scratch-building. Space Shuttle kits are mostly available in 1:144 scale, especially

from Airfix and Revell, though what was originally G-Mark, and now Minicraft, also makes a full stack Shuttle kit.

Project Constellation would have used two types of launcher: Ares I that carried crews and little else, and Ares V that was uncrewed and carried the heavier payloads.

Ares I is the smaller and simpler as it is basically a single Shuttle SRB with a new upper stage. However, the SRB has an extra segment added from the Shuttle set-up, bringing the total to five. If you are just building Ares I, one Shuttle kit will supply two SRBs, so the extra segment can be added from that. Building the Ares V will require two complete kits, as you will need four SRBs in total – plus the ET for the Ares V is also lengthened, so this would also require two kits. However, if the SRB segments are juggled between the Ares I and V, you can get away building both launchers with two full stack Shuttle kits.

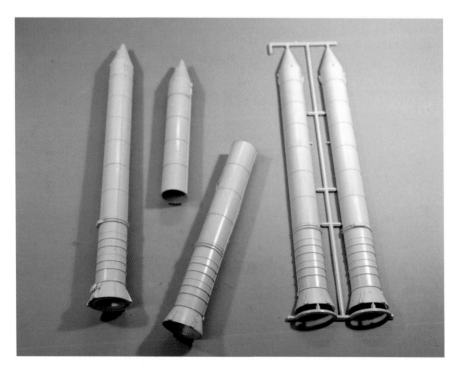

A selection of SRBs for the conversion into the Ares I launcher.

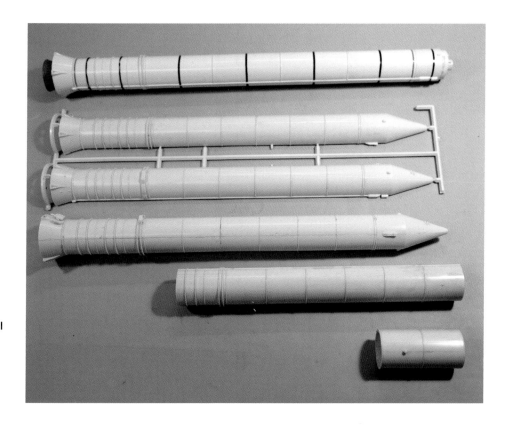

Lining up original SRBs against the completed Ares I version – top. These are longer by one segment.

Building Ares I

Starting with the first stage, in theory the two SRBs can be assembled, and then cut and extended. However, because the finished model is going to be somewhat top heavy – the upper stage is wider than the first stage – some method of support is best dealt with first. A support in the shape of a ¼in (7.5mm) steel rod is suitable. Cut two circles of fairly thick plastic sheet that will fit the inner diameter of the SRBs, and drill a suitable hole in each, to match the rod. Better still, find a tube (such as EMA VT-14) that will slide over the steel rod, and then drill the holes in the support discs to fit this. The support rod then only has to slide up the tubing, you don't have to juggle it into individual holes. Cement the whole ensemble inside the SRB half, one just above where the rocket nozzle will fit, and the other to at least where the SRB will be cut for the lengthening.

For the addition of the extra SRB segment, mark the circular line below the uppermost twin circular strips, themselves just below the nose cone. Line up the other SRB so that the overall length is increased by one segment. As it is only one segment, it could be an ideal chance to use up odd lengths of SRBs that may be in the bits and pieces box. The SRB nose cone is not required, so that too can be removed. For added strength, the two SRB halves could be 'staggered', so if you use this method, cut the two halves one segment apart. When the halves are then glued together this will strengthen the whole structure.

With the lengthened SRB, the supplied engine plate and engine cone are fitted in place. If a support rod is being used, the engine bell also needs an appropriate hole drilled through its centre.

The upper stage is a wider diameter, and here based round an EMA tube, 1³/₈in (36mm) in diameter (EMA number VT-40), cut to a length of

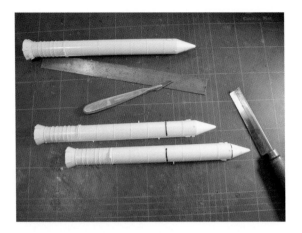

Marking two Airfix SRBs as to where the cuts will be to gain one extra segment. Note this is below the uppermost segment, as that has the double rings.

Fitting rings cut from plastic sheet, and an inner EMA pipe (tube) inside the SRB half, to take the ¼in (6mm) steel support rod. The discs were cut with the hole cutter – far right. The central hole was then drilled out to ¼in diameter. (This is for one of the pair for the Ares V, but the Ares I is exactly the same procedure.)

The components for the Ares I, before painting. Top is the upper stage, below that the Orion command module, topped with the launch escape system. The lengthened SRB is below these.

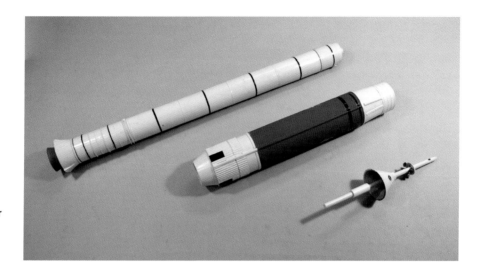

The finished components – top: SRB; centre: the upper stage; bottom: the Orion and launch escape system.

6.5in (170mm). These EMA tubes are not cheap, and these days, with the introduction of so much being 3D printed, may not be easy to find. But as Project Constellation was never built, an exact match is less important than if it had been built, so something close in diameter is equally suitable. Even cardboard tubes can be used. Card tube is usually fairly strong and the surface can be made easier to finish and paint by wrapping thin plastic sheet round the card, held in place by aerosol adhesive, available at DIY and arts and crafts stores. Alternatively, seal with sanding sealer (intended for building balsawood models): this will seal the card allowing the usual paints to be used.

Building the Upper Stage

This stage is wider than the SRB diameter, so it needs a connection. Conveniently, the conical lower section of the SRB, the skirt, is an almost exact match. It obviously matches the SRB at the lower end as that is where it is originally attached. But the SRB is the same diameter along its length, so it matches the diameter at the top end as well. Consequently it is used here, but upside-down.

First cut off this cone and remove the four SRB hold-down bolt connectors, though they could be left in place as 'details'. (Actually these were the only

points that held the whole full stack Shuttle to the pad, via 3.5in (89mm) diameter explosive bolts!) Next, invert and cement the matching diameter end to the top of the lengthened SRB. You may find that some additional support inside – a ring of plastic sheet, for example – could be necessary to add strength. The alternative is to use the inverted lower section with the cone as the 'lengthened' part of the SRB, though this has six circular rings moulded in around the section, which are not on the drawing of the proposed Ares I – but as we are back to this hardware never having been built, it could be a quicker option.

Although the main diameter of the upper stage is $1^3/_8$in (36mm) in diameter, the uppermost section is truncated down to 1¼in (32mm) in diameter, for an added length of $1^9/_{16}$in (39mm); so geometrically this section is a very narrow cone.

As with many projects in these pages, 'cones' come into rocket building quite a lot, and a number can be found in commercial kits, especially for such as the Saturn V. The top of the S-II stage is a cone that attaches to the S-IVB stage, and above that, the SLA, which houses the Lunar Module, is also conical. Other cone shapes are available from commercial suppliers, particularly EMA. The cone here, though, is very steep in cross-section: it would have an angle at the apex of only around 10 degrees, which is far less than more standard cones where the angles might be 60 and 90 degrees. However, there are two ways to make a cone. If you have the skills (and a wood-turning lathe) it could be turned from wood.

Alternatively, cut the thinner tube long enough to slide into the thicker tube, leaving a suitable length that is the basis of the 'cone'. The conical shape can then be traced out on a sheet of thin – such as 0.5mm – plastic sheet using a set of compasses, and the sheet cut with scissors. Then bend it round, glue it into place, and conceal and strengthen the join with a plastic strip. Given that this design was never built, the odd strip added is not going against any actual design. If you wish, this can be matched with another strip 180 degrees round, and even ones at 90 degrees to these.

Building Orion

The top section is the crewed spacecraft, basically the same Orion craft that has ended up at the top of Artemis. It is basically a larger Apollo, capable of carrying more crew, though it has the same profile. The conical angle is – from a modelling point of view – virtually a right angle, so 90 degrees. Being larger, using a Command Module (CM) from a 1:144-scale Apollo kit isn't viable, though of course you could use a larger scale than 1:144, the nearest of which would be the 1:96 scale from Revell. But this is too big, so would need cutting down from the heat-shield end. Arguably it is easier to use different parts, and here the 90-degree EMA cones could be an answer. These come with a separate

Slotting the SRB over the steel rod, fixed to a purpose-built MDF base. The model needs some support like this, otherwise it is top heavy.

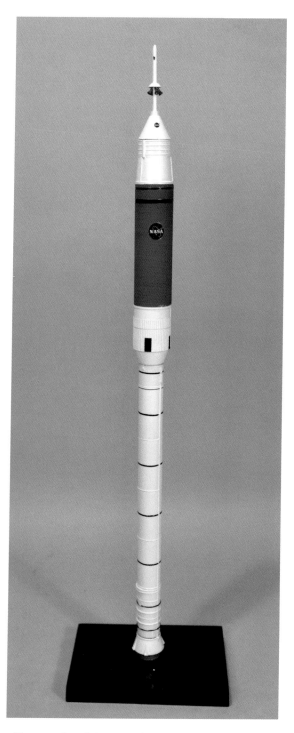

The completed Ares I on its custom base. Note the upper stage would likely use cryogenic fuels, so has the 'ET foam' on it.

top section, which has a diameter of just about 1¼in (32mm), so is an easy modification as it just matches the top of the second stage.

As with Apollo, there is a launch escape system, which again could be adapted from an Apollo kit – but in 1:144 scale, these are really too thin. The next up in scale are the 1:96 Revell and 1:72-scale Dragon kits, but of course these are the opposite – really too thick. The best compromise is new tube, here again an EMA part, $^3/_{16}$in (5mm) (tube part P (-) 6), with a rounded end. Fill the end with modelling putty or filler, and once thoroughly dry, sand to a suitable blunt cone.

The rocket engines that would lift the spacecraft in a launch emergency were made from four nozzles salvaged from another kit and fitted to another EMA part, actually a conical-shaped lampshade, code LF-12. But as with most of these builds, precise measurements are unimportant, so a search in that bits and pieces box could bring up alternatives.

Most of these rocket sections have vertical corrugations at some point along their length (the Saturn V has a number of them). The Ares I is shown with a short length at the bottom of the second stage, which can be reproduced by using one of the after-market corrugated plastic sheets available. The upper section, below the Orion, has circular rings, which can be cut from plastic strip, or alternatively adapted from the lower section of a spare SRB.

Note, if you are sliding the inner tube into the outer, and the fit isn't quite snug enough, wrap some thin plastic sheet around the end of the inner tube, until you get the correct thickness.

Building Ares V

The launcher is basically a Space Shuttle booster section, with lengthened SRBs and a lengthened External Tank. The payload section then sits on top of the ET.

However, the ET cannot feed the SSMEs of the Orbiter as there isn't one. Instead, a number of rocket engines were planned to be fitted under the ET, fed from the liquid hydrogen and liquid oxygen tanks in the ET. The actual engines wavered between six RS-68 engines (developed for the Delta IV launcher), or five RS-25 engines – otherwise known as SSMEs. Consequently, take your pick! Five engines fit better; four arranged at right-angles to each other, and one in the centre, as in the Saturn V. Here a compromise was made by using the second-stage engines from the S-II stage of an Airfix Saturn V and their mounting plates. The engine bells are somewhat undersize (for SSMEs), but again, this set-up was never built, so this would be acceptable.

The outer section of this engine package was built by cutting down the conical section from the Saturn V S-II stage, covered with the fairings that come with

Marking up the top section of an External Tank that will form the top of the Ares V. The lower section needs removing as the upper stage is a smaller diameter than the External Tank itself.

Forming the upper section of the new External Tank, with its corrugated 'reducer'.

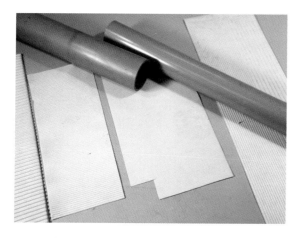

Examples of various 'corrugated' embossed plastic sheet, used as 'wraps' around various stages on this, and many other builds.

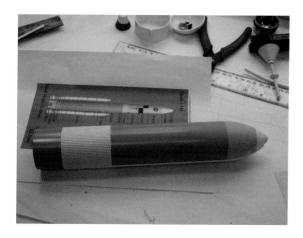

The upper payload section of Ares V, showing here that the nose cone is turned wood, with the topmost section in styrene.

strip of plastic, and cut the rounded bottom off the lower section. The engine section fits here. The LOX pipe could be made by cutting and joining two kit parts, though frankly it is easier just to make a new one-piece pipe of a similar diameter.

Using the corrugated embossed plastic sheet, three sections of the ET were covered, though again the exact length and position of each is not vital.

The upper stage of the set-up is depicted slightly thinner than the ET. (It would have been a lot easier to model if the external diameter were the same

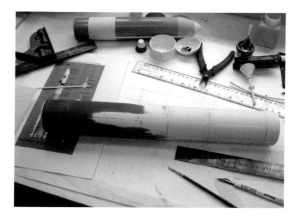

Starting the 'foam' finish on the ET section of the Ares V.

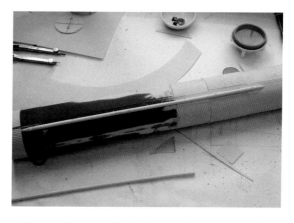

More on the foam finish for the ET. A new conduit has been added – this is from the larger 1:72 Monogram External Tank, though any half-section of tube will suffice.

the Heller Ariane 4 kit, trimmed to fit over the four outer engine bells.

The External Tank requires two Shuttle kits, because at around 16in (400mm) it is longer than a standard Shuttle tank. The exact cutting points are not that vital, but ensure the fairings for the external liquid oxygen pipe are retained top and bottom, and make sure that the final length ends up at 16in (400mm). Join the two tank sections together with an internal

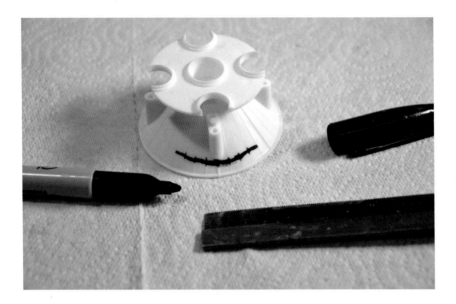

The beginnings of the new engine section for the Ares V that will sit under the External Tank (as there is no Orbiter). It is cut from the engine bulkhead of the S-II stage for the Airfix Saturn V kit.

The fairings round the outer engine bells are taken from the Heller 1:125-scale Ariane 4 kit.

all the way up – it would just have needed three ETs!) However, the upper section is 2in (50mm) in diameter, which is only a ¼in (6mm) smaller than the ET diameter. This used more EMA tube (VT-200), cut to around 9½in (240mm) long. This diameter difference means that a conical section is needed to join these two sections; however, the upper 2in (50mm) diameter section just about fits inside the 2¼in (56mm) diameter ET, so maybe with slight packing this will fit without any more work.

However, it does leave a section on the outer surface that needs to be a cone, but because the

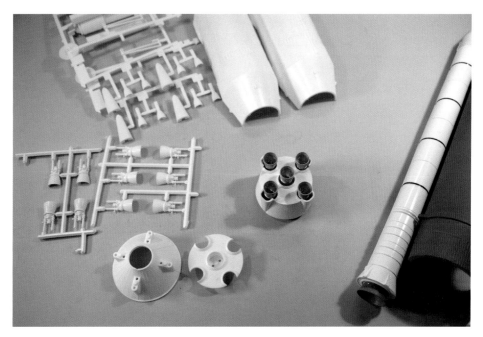

The various components for the engine section, taken from the Airfix Saturn V kit, left, with the finished part at the centre. The first stage of the Ares V is on the right, with the lower section of the ET removed, ready to receive the engines.

difference each side is only $^1/_8$in (3mm), and this section would have been corrugated, this can be achieved by cutting two sections of the embossed plastic sheet and cementing them in place separately. Any prominent gaps can be covered with plastic strip, maybe half-round mouldings. There are more corrugations about this for around $2^3/_8$in (58mm), but as this isn't a cone, a one-piece strip of 'corrugations' can be used.

The nose cone of the payload stage is conveniently the same profile as the top of the original ET, so one choice is to use this. However, it will need the lower end cutting down with a razor saw, so the diameter matches the tube – that is, from 2¼in (56mm) down to 2in (50mm). The rest of the nose cone can be used 'as is' – not forgetting the tip that is moulded as a separate part in the Airfix kit, though not in the Revell. Alternatively, the nose cone can be sanded from a wooden plug, which was the method used here. Once sealed, primed and painted, it is really impossible to tell how the nose cone was made.

Building the Long SRBs

The SRBs of the Ares V can be lengthened in the same way as the single one for the Ares I, though here the nose cones are retained. Fitting the SRBs to the ET could be the same as supplied in the kits, but – as detailed in Chapter 10 – although fine in high tensile metal and full size, in 1:144 and in styrene, these are fairly weak. A better option is to attach the SRBs to the ET directly. Drill through the ET, making sure the opposite holes match up, at least approximately! Then drill matching holes in the SRBs.

Pass a length of thick plastic rod, or thin metal through the ET, leaving enough either side to go into the SRBs. A useful 'pipe' is EMA's thinnest 'plastic' pipe, which is actually plastic-coated metal rod. These have the advantage of having the strength of the metal, but the outer layer – the plastic – will glue with styrene cement. There are two sizes P-(-)-1 and P-(-)-2. (The centre (-) is to put in the plastic colour – but (W) is usual as it is white!)

What would be the lower attachments point can then be visually added, either using the original parts supplied in the kit, or making up new ones from more lengths of the plastic-coated rods.

The completed Ares V. The black squares come from a black decal sheet.

As with the Ares I, if you want a support stand, the cleanest method is via the SRBs as it won't show how the model is sitting on a base. Fit internal guide rods inside the SRBs before the halves are joined. The bases here were cut from MDF, sealed and spray-painted Humbrol Midnight Blue.

Finishes for the Ares I and V

Both the Ares I and V were white, with the External Tank of the V and the upper stage of the Ares I covered with the same insulation foam as used on the full stack Shuttle. As this is actually the unpainted foam – so not paint – and is not smooth, as a paint finish, it has always been a slight problem to match, not only in colour, but also in texture. With care a 'rough' surface could be hand painted, by adding some fine material to paint, but this would be really fine.

However, there are textured spray paints available. Testors did make a textured paint intended to reproduce the vinyl roofs of car models. Unfortunately the range of Testor paints has been much reduced over the years, and this is now unavailable (though older spray cans were used on these models). But there is a wide range of general household aerosols available in DIY and craft stores, some that feature 'textured' colours, so one of these could be an option.

The actual foam colour is extremely unlikely to be available, and anyway varies from one ET to another. So prime the tank with white or a light colour, then top with a variation of the foam colour. The closest straight out of an aerosol can are Humbrol 29 Dark Brown and Testor FS30140 Light Earth, though neither are really correct. (The Testor is slightly closer as it is 'redder'.) Frankly the colour will have to be decided by eye and mixed. Most of the examples here used Humbrol 186 as the main colour, lightened somewhat with Matt White, 34, with a touch of a dark red, 73, to give a slight reddish tinge. But the foam on the real Shuttle tanks appeared a multitude of shades, so either copy one of those, or work on the principle that most models of 'proposals' would

What would have been Project Constellation: the crewed Ares I (left) and uncrewed Ares V.

be somewhat simplified, and the foam (or anything else) would be one colour all over the relevant areas. So whatever shade you mix, either apply it thin and via an air-brush, or hand-paint it.

Incidentally, the vast majority of paints used in the home are now acrylic based, so there should not be any compatibility problems – but as always in these matters, if you are unsure, test first! (Removing acrylic paint once dry, if it is wrong, is far more difficult than removing older enamel paints. Consequently the rule is to 'get it right the first time' so you don't have to remove the paint!)

The finishing touches for both launchers are the markings. The SRBs would likely have black lines round the segments, so reproduce these with thin strips from aftermarket decal sheets. The larger black segments (roll patterns) on the upper stage of Ares V can be cut from stock black decal sheet, while 'USA', 'UNITED STATES' and the Stars and Stripes can come from existing space kits. The NASA Meatballs are also in some kits, such as the Space Shuttle, and are also available on specialist decal sheets from such as RealSpace Models and New Ware.

APPENDIX
THE MODEL COMPANIES

Model companies can very simply be split into two definitions: 'Mainstream' and 'Specialist'.

'Mainstream' refers to companies that produce kits in injection styrene, which would normally be found in hobby stores and model shops.

'Specialist' indicates what are usually one-person operations that produce all subjects of kits in all types of materials – *except* injection styrene – and which are normally only available from specialist hobby shops and/or by mail direct from the company's web site.

MAINSTREAM COMPANIES

ACADEMY

(www.academyhobby.com)
Academy Plastic Model Co Ltd, 521-1, Yonghyeon-dong, Uijeangbu-si, Gyeonggi-du, South Korea

The major Korean model producer that used to work with Minicraft in the USA, though that connection was severed in 1997. It issued various Space Shuttle kits in 1:288 scale.

AIRFIX

(www.airfix.com)
Hornby Hobbies Ltd, Margate, Kent CT9 4JX, UK

One of the first model kit companies, and still one of the best known names world-wide. Over the years it produced a wide range of subjects, particularly aircraft and a reasonable range of space rockets. Now owned by Hornby, along with Humbrol, Corgi, Scalextric and Hornby Railways.

AMT

(www.round2models.com/models/amt)
Round 2 Models, 4073 Meghan Beeler Drive, South Bend, IN 46628, USA

One of the original American model companies, best known for its car models. It then introduced the first Star Trek kits, and its famous five-piece 'Man in Space' set. Having been taken over by Lesney, it was then acquired by Ertl, which itself was taken over by RC2 (Racing Champions). Consequently it joined its original rival, MPC, as that had also been bought by Ertl. Both companies were then acquired by the new Round 2 company in 2009.

AOSHIMA

(www.aoshima-bk.co.jp)
Aoshima Bunka Kyozai Co Ltd, 12-3 Ryutsu Centre, Shizuoka City, Japan 420

One of the oldest model companies in the world, with beginnings in the 1920s making wooden kits. Moved to plastic in the early 1960s and is still producing a wide range of models. Produced an early range of Apollo-related models and in recent years a brand new range of Japanese satellites.

ATLANTIS MODELS

(www.atlantis-models.com)
Atlantis Toy and Hobby Inc., 435 Brook Avenue Unit-16, Deer Park, NY 11729, USA

Founded in 2009 by the former owners of Megahobby.com, Peter Vetri and Rick DelFavero. Initially issued kits of its own series of 'flying saucers'. In early 2018, acquired much of the Revell-Monogram,

Aurora and Renwal tooling, when the Revell Group stopped trading after the Hobbico collapse. Has issued a number of Revell space and missile kits.

BANDAI

(www.bandai-hobby.net)

Bandai Co Ltd, 5-4 2-chome, Komagata, Taito-ku, Tokyo, Japan

Well known Japanese toy manufacturer that has also made kits over the years. Many are classic Japanese anime characters, though it has also made more traditional modelling subjects, including some space subjects.

DOYUSHA

(www.doyusha-model.com)

Doyusha Model Co Ltd., 4-27-21, Arakawa, Arakawa-ku, Tokyo, Japan

One of the older Japanese names, still in production with a wide range of kits, including some that are space oriented.

DRAGON

(www.dragon-models.com)

Dragon Models Ltd, B1, 10/F, Kong Nam Industrial Building, 603-609 Castle Peak Road, Tsuen Wan New Territories, Hong Kong

Producer of aircraft, military and a new range of Apollo-based space kits.

HASEGAWA

(www.hasegawa-model.co.jp)

Hasegawa Seisakuso Co Ltd, 3-1-2 Yagusu Yaizu Shizuoka 425-8711, Japan

One of the major Japanese kit companies with a wide range of subjects, military, aircraft, cars, ships and airliners. Has issued Shuttle kits in 1:200 scale.

HELLER

(www.heller.fr)

Heller Joustra SA, Chemin de la Porte, 61160 Trun, France

Founded in 1957 by Léo Jahiel. Since then the company has been through several ownerships, including being joined to Airfix when both were owned by Humbrol. However, it was not acquired along with Airfix and Humbrol when they were bought by Hornby, and Heller now runs as an independent company. It issues kits across the range of aircraft, ships and galleons, and cars. Using its own (unique) 1:125 scale, issued Ariane rockets and the ISS.

HORIZON MODELS

(www.horizon-models.com)

Horizon Models Pty Ltd, PO Box 305, Drummoyne NSW 2047, Australia

A new company started by Tony Radosevic in 2015, with its first kits dealing with early American space subjects, including the Mercury launchers.

ITALERI

(www.italeri.com)

Italeri S.p.A., via Pradazzo, 6/b, 1-40012 Calderara di Reno, Bologna, Italy

Began in 1960s and has gone through two name changes. It was originally Artiplast, but this was changed to Italereri, then to the simplified Italeri. In recent years it took over former Italian rivals ESCI (acquired from Ertl) and Protar, and works in conjunction with Testors and Revell. Makes a wide range of kit subjects. Acquired some AMT-originated aircraft, including the XB-70.

MINICRAFT

(www.minicraftmodels.com)

Minicraft Models (US) Inc, 1501 Commerce Drive, Elgin IL 60123, USA

Started by Al Trendle in 1970 as a US importer of Japanese kits, Minicraft now designs and issues many of its own kits. Issued the Space Shuttle Full Stack kit originated by G-Mark.

MONOGRAM

See: REVELL and MONOGRAM

MPC

(www.round2models.com/models/mpc)

Round 2 Models, 4073 Meghan Beeler Drive, South Bend, IN 46628, USA

Similar to AMT, MPC was created in the 1960s to make model car kits. It became famous for producing the first Star Wars kits. It was acquired by Round 2 in 2009. It issued a few space-oriented kits, including the Pilgrim Observer space station.

MRC

(www.modelrectifier.com)

Model Rectifier Corp, 80 Newfield Avenue, Eldon, NJ 08837, USA

An importer of kits for the US market, including many from Academy and Italeri. Issued Atomic City's 1:12 scale Mercury spacecraft kit.

REVELL and MONOGRAM

(www.revell.de / www.revell.com)

Revell GmbH & Co. KG, Henschelstrasse 20-30, D-32257, Bünde, Germany

Revell USA LLC, 728, Northwest Highway, Ste 302, Fox River Grove, IL 60021, USA

Two of the best-known names in modelling, combined since 1986. Both companies have issued many model kits, including many space and missile kits. Revell had acquired the Renwal name and tooling, and Monogram much of the Aurora tooling. R-M was acquired by the large hobby distribution company Hobbico, in 2007. Revell-Germany ran very much as an independent company, although was eventually acquired by Hobbico in 2011. Hobbico went into liquidation in early 2018, but Germany was in a better position than Revell-Monogram for recovery. Revell-Germany was taken over by the German company Blitz in mid-2018, which also acquired the American side. This consequently moved the main headquarters for the whole company to Europe.

SPECIAL HOBBY

(www.specialhobby.eu)

Special Hobby, s.r.o., Mezilesí 718/78, 193 00 Prague, Czech Republic

Borders between being a mainstream and a specialist company, and includes MPM and CMK ranges. Produces a wide range of aircraft and military items, including several scales of the X-15.

TAMIYA

(www.tamiya.com)

Tamiya inc., 307 Ondawara, Suruga-Ku, Shizuoka 422-8610, Japan

One of the major Japanese model companies and arguably the best known. Created in 1948 by Shunska Tamiya, initially making wooden ship kits, only later moving to plastic. Tamiya's ranges encompass most modelling subjects and it has large radio control, robotic and educational model divisions. Produces the 1:100 scale Space Shuttle Orbiter.

UNION

Union Model Co Ltd, No 26.8, 3 Chome, Umejima, Adachi-Ku, Tokyo, Japan

Produced a range of models, some re-boxed from US originals. Began the range of 1:288 Space Shuttle kits, re-boxed by Revell and other companies.

SPECIALIST COMPANIES

ANIGRAND CRAFTSWORK

(www.anigrand.com)

Flat F, 23 Floor, Block 4, Waterside Plaza, Wing Shun Street, Tune Wan, NT, Hong Kong

Specialist producer of resin kits, featuring a number of aircraft, space and X-plane subjects.

ATOMIC CITY

(www.atomiccitymodels.com)

Atomic City Engineering, Hanford, CA 93230, USA

Atomic City makes short runs of SF subjects plus the 1:12 scale injection styrene kit of the Mercury Capsule; distributed though MRC. (*See* also MRC in the Mainstream listing.)

FANTASTIC PLASTIC

(www.fantastic-plastic.com)

Fantastic Plastic Models, LLC, 25501 Willow Wood Street, Lake Forest, CA 92630, USA

Founded by Allen Ury and produces a wide range of space-oriented kits.

NEW WARE

(mek.kosmo.cz/newware)

Zelazneho 6, 71200 Ostava 2, Czech Republic

Producer of many specialist accessory sets for space modellers to update such kits as Revell's International Space Station and Mir kit, plus complete kits of Soviet/Russian craft such as Soyuz and Vostok. Run by Tomas Kladiva.

REALSPACE MODELS

(www.realspacemodels.com)

813 Watt Drive, Tallahassee, FL 32303, USA

RealSpace Models, founded by Glenn Johnson, has the largest range of specialist material spacecraft kits in the USA, making everything from a 1:200 Skylab adaptor for the AMT Saturn 5 kit, to Voyager, Viking and Magellan spaceprobes in 1:24 scale. Also made are detailing sets and decal sheets. The company distributes the detailed plans of David Weeks.

SHARKITS

(www.sharkit.com)

9 rue de la Picardière, 78200 Perdreauville, France

Founded by Franck 'Sharky' Wagner to make specialist aerospace subjects, mostly in resin. The range includes several missiles, and a variation on the X-15.

GENERAL SUPPLIERS

BARE-METAL FOIL

(www.bare-metal.com)

Bare Metal Foil Co, PO Box 82, Farmington, MI 48332, USA

Producer of Bare-Metal Foil, and other modelling accessories.

EMA and PLASTRUCT

(www.plastruct.com\www.ema-models.co.uk)

Engineering Model Associates, 1020 S. Wallace Place, City of Industry, CA 91748, USA

EMA Model Supplies Ltd, 14 Beadman Street, London SE27 0DN, UK

EMA is the major producer of specialist model parts made initially for professional modellers of chemical plant models and the like. However, it can be adapted to a wide range of modelling projects from the special effects industry to the hobbyist. For the last, the division 'Plastruct' was introduced to supply the smaller ranges of EMA parts.

HUMBROL

(www.humbrol.com)

Hornby Hobbies Ltd, Margate, Kent CT9 4JX, UK

The UK's major model paint manufacturer. Founded in 1919 in Kingston upon Hull as the Humber Oil Company. It moved into modelling paints, then other accessories, from the 1950s and became Humbrol. Acquired by Borden in 1976, that also at the time owned Heller. Acquired by Hornby in 2006.

MR HOBBY

(www.mr-hobby.com)

GSI Creos Corporation, 2-3-1, Kudan Minami, Chiyoda-ku, Tokyo, 102-0074, Japan

Major Japanese producer of hobby paints and accessories. The overall company was initially created in 1931, and became Gunze Sangyo in 1971. Changed to GSI Creos in 2001. Has used the Gunze Sangyo name in the past, for both paints and model kits. Now uses the 'Mr Hobby' name for all hobby-related items.

TESTORS

(www.testors.com)

The Testor Corporation, 440 Blackhawk Park Avenue, Rockford, IL 61104, USA

America's main model paint and accessory supplier, Testors also issued kits from companies it has acquired over the years, including Hawk and IMC. It also produced a series of UFO kits of its own. Most kit names and tooling have now been acquired by Round 2.

DISTRIBUTORS

Even with the demise of many model shops and hobby stores around the world, some do fortunately remain, and many have moved over to online and mail order. It is impossible to list all distributors here – try a web search – but below are some where the author has personal experience or recommendations.

CULT TV MAN SHOP

(www.culttvmanshop.com)
CultTVMan, 248 E. Crogan St, Suite 202, Lawrenceville, GA 30046, USA
Proprietor: Steve Iverson.
Very wide section of all types of science fiction, fantasy and factual space kits, plus accessories.

FEDERATION MODELS

(www.federationmodels.com)
PO Box 110796, Palm Bay, FL 32911-0796, USA
Supplier of many multi-material science fiction kits.

HANNANTS

(www.hannants.co.uk)
H.G. Hannant Ltd, Harbour Road, Oulton Broad, Lowestoft, Suffolk NR32 3LR, UK
Proprietor: Nigel Hannant.
UK's largest model kit distributor, specialising primarily in aircraft and military. Many decals and accessory sets, and its own paint ranges.

HOBBY BOUNTIES

(www.hobbybounties.com)
Hobby Bounties & Morgan Hobbycraft Centre, 865 Mountbatten Road #0291/92, Katong Shopping Centre, Singapore 437844, Republic of Singapore
Proprietor: Peter Chiang
Large general hobby supply shop. Also owner of the FROG name.

HOBBY LINK JAPAN

(www.hlj.com)
Hobby Link Japan Ltd, Tatebayashi-shi, Nishitakane-cho 43-6, Gunma 374-0075, Japan
Proprietor: Scott T. Hards
Excellent source for Japanese kits, tools and accessories. Mail-order world-wide.

MODELS FOR SALE LTD

(www.modelsforsale.com)
Unit 3, Dean Close, Raunds, Northants NN9 6BD, UK
Proprietor: Vince Brown.
Specialist kit supplier, including paints. Mail order and some UK model shows.

SQUADRON

(www.squadron.com)
Squadron, 1115 Crowley Drive, Carrollton, TX 75006-1313, USA
Originally created in 1968 in Detroit, Squadron is one of America's major model distribution companies, dealing with hobby products from around the world, including kits, accessories and tools. It uses the ENCORE MODELS name for its own kits.

STARSHIP MODELER

(www.starshipmodeler.com)
PO Box 549, Lake Villa, IL 60046, USA
Proprietor: John Lester.
Mainly SF, plus paint, tools, books and magazines.

TIMELESS HOBBIES (was COMET MINIATURES)

(www.timeless-hobbies.com)
Timeless Hobbies Ltd, Unit 6, Leys Farm, Chelmsford Road, High Ongar, Essex CM5 9NW, UK
Proprietor: Tony James.
The UK's largest specialist science fiction model, toy and 'collectible' supplier.

EBAY

(www.ebay.com / www.ebay.co.uk etc.)
And finally, even if after all these you still cannot locate something you need, you may just have to resort to eBay.

RESEARCH AND THE WEB

These days when considering research, it is very easy to say that it'll all be found 'on the 'net'. To a great extent this is true, though with the proviso that sometimes there is too much information on the Internet, and sorting what you want from want you don't, is not always straightforward and in many cases can lead to extreme frustration! However, do not forget that good old-fashioned paper references (books and magazines) still have their important role to play. Plus, even these days, not everyone has a computer, tablet or smartphone with direct access to the Internet, though connections are found everywhere in schools, colleges, community centres, libraries and Internet cafés.

OTHER USEFUL SITES

Here are various International Plastic Modellers' websites from around the world:
 UK: www.ipmsuk.org
 US: www.ipmsusa.org
 Canada: www.ipmscanada.org
 Australia: www.ipmsaustralia.com.au
 New Zealand: ipmsnz.hobbyvista.com
Most other countries follow similar syntax, or use a search engine.
 Scale Model News: www.scalemodelnews.com
 Model Stories: modelstories.free.fr (*en francais*)
 Milano Model and Toy Museum: www.toys-n-cars.com
 The author's site is: www.matirvine.com

Note also that most web sites also have many links to other relevant pages.

INDEX

First published in 2024 by
The Crowood Press Ltd
Ramsbury, Marlborough
Wiltshire SN8 2HR

enquiries@crowood.com

www.crowood.com

This impression 2024

British Library Cataloguing-in-Publication Data
A catalogue record for this book is available from the
British Library.

ISBN 978 0 7198 4320 4

Mat Irvine and David Baker have asserted their right under
the Copyright, Designs and Patents Act 1988 to be identified as the authors of this work.

Typeset by Envisage IT
Cover design Blue Sunflower Creative
Printed and bound in India by Parksons Graphics Pvt. Ltd.

Dedication
To Martin Postranecky. An old friend of both authors, and
a fellow Fellow of the British Interplanetary Society, Martin
combines an interest of space history and spacecraft model
making.

Image credits
Ball Brothers: p.26 (top)

Boeing: p.114

Martin Marietta: p.158 (top and bottom), p.159

McDonnell: p.17, p.18, p.41, p.42, p.53

NASA: p.16, p.40, p.52, p.67, p.68, p.82, p.83, p.84,
p.85, p.96, p.97, p.98, p.99, p.129 (bottom), p.144
(top and bottom), p.157, p.170, p.171 (top and bottom)

North American: p.113 (top and bottom)

USAF: p.54, p.55, p.69